# LAMENTATIONS

# THE OLD TESTAMENT LIBRARY

Editorial Advisory Board

Adele Berlin

# Lamentations

## A Commentary

Westminster John Knox Press
LOUISVILLE • LONDON

*Book design by Jennifer K. Cox*

*First paperback edition*
Published by Westminster John Knox Press
Louisville, Kentucky

This book is printed on acid-free paper that meets the American National Standards Institute Z39.48 standard. ∞

PRINTED IN THE UNITED STATES OF AMERICA

**Library of Congress Cataloging-in-Publication Data**
A catalog record for this book is available from the Library of Congress.

ISBN 0-664-22974-3

לאיתן דוד
נצחי ותוחלתי

# CONTENTS

# PREFACE

While Lamentations has received its share of exegesis, it is surprising that a text as rich as this one in poetic attributes has received so little literary attention, aside from studies of its formal structures. The vivid imagery and abundance of metaphors cry out for explication, for it is largely in the images, the multi-faceted associations that they evoke, and the movement of the discourse that the meaning of the book resides. This commentary will concentrate on these literary aspects of the book, but not solely for their aesthetic value. Behind the metaphors and other literary tropes lies a conceptual world of religious beliefs. One of my goals is to discover the religious worldview that informs the imagery of the book and to explicate the imagery in light of that worldview. Frames of reference such as the concept of purity, mourning, repentance, and the Davidic covenant are useful in this effort.

I will not belabor the historical background against which the poems are set, although I will mention it when it helps to clarify a reference. Lamentations is certainly not the best historical source for the destruction of Jerusalem, and was never intended as such. It assumes knowledge of the events leading up to and following the destruction, but it has its own way of presenting them and its own purpose for doing so, and we should try to fathom why the book puts things the way it does.

Historical-critical questions will also be slighted, not because they are unimportant, but because there is little evidence to pinpoint either the absolute or the relative dating of the individual chapters or their parts. We have no information on how the book came to be composed, except that it seems likely that the five chapters once existed as independent poems.

A commentary need not be encyclopedic. I have not attempted to represent every interpretation put forth or every issue debated in the scholarly literature. Indeed, a commentary gets its character from what is selected for comment, both from the text and from the secondary literature. That is why there are, and can be, so many commentaries. My approach is literary, with emphasis on understanding the poetic discourse, vocabulary, and imagery of the Masoretic Text. Toward this goal, I often compare the passage in question with other biblical passages and with extrabiblical sources from the ancient Near East. These comparisons reveal what in Lamentations is conventional and what is innovative, and they shed light on the broader cultural context from which the book emerged and in which it should be understood. Philological, grammatical, and text-critical issues will, of course, be dealt with, but not at length if previous commentaries have already addressed them adequately. Questions of poetic form and structure—types of parallelism, word patterns, acrostics, meter— have lost their urgency, having been studied so much in the last thirty years. The form-critical question of whether Lamentations belongs to the genre of communal lament, funeral dirge, or some combination of the two goes back to the work of Hedwig Jahnow, and was developed considerably by Claus Westermann, and more recently by Erhard Gerstenberger. We seem to be at an impasse on this question, which suggests that it may be more productive to consider the issue of genre from a different perspective. Another issue that has been debated for some time, without resolution, is the degree of influence of the Sumerian city laments on biblical laments. Both genre and Mesopotamian influence remain important issues, and can be usefully discussed together, as in the monograph by F. W. Dobbs-Allsopp, *Weep, O Daughter of Zion*. In fact, Lamentations should be studied in an even wider literary context, beyond lament literature (see Introduction, Lamentations in Literary Context).

Feminist criticism is now an accepted form of biblical study in the academy, and a branch of it is related to literary criticism. While there is not a large body of feminist work on Lamentations, the work on prophetic literature and some of the general observations and issues that feminist interpretation has raised are usefully applied to the interpretation of Lamentations. This is not a feminist commentary per se, but it will draw on some feminist interpretation of the female imagery that is so prominent in the book.

Quite a number of new studies of Lamentations have appeared during the last decade or so, representing a variety of interpretive approaches, and they form the scholarly context in which this volume was written. They include the commentaries of F. W. Dobbs-Allsopp, E. Gerstenberger, D. Hillers, Y. Z. Moskowitz, K. O'Connor (*NIB*), I. Provan, and J. Renkema, and the monographs of F. W. Dobbs-Allsopp, J. Hunter, N. C. Lee, T. Linafelt, X. H. T. Pham, and C. Westermann. Their influence on my understanding of Lamentations is more pervasive than specific acknowledgments can document. These recent works testify to the increasing interest in literary matters (broadly defined) that characterizes much recent biblical exegesis, but none privileges literary interpretation to the degree that the present commentary does. Its emphasis is on finding new insights into passages whose meaning and literary effect was never fully plumbed before.

I am grateful to Chip Dobbs-Allsopp, Ed Greenstein, Magnar Kartveit, Jacob Klein, Nancy C. Lee, and Kathleen O'Connor for making available to me their unpublished work. Special thanks to Kathleen O'Connor and Chip

Dobbs-Allsopp for access to their commentaries prior to their publication. I had the privilege of teaching Lamentations to students at the Baltimore Hebrew University and at MaTan in Jerusalem. Their questions and observations pushed me to make more sense of the text, and they served as a sounding board for some of my interpretations. I thank the editors of the Old Testament Library series for the invitation to write this volume and Carey C. Newman, Senior Editor for Academic Books at Westminster John Knox Press, for shepherding the book through the publication process. A special word of gratitude to Carol Newsom, the editor of this volume, who read the manuscript with great care and offered sage advice on many points. The volume has been the beneficiary of her considerable knowledge and her consummate good sense. My undergraduate assistants at the University of Maryland, Abbey Bittel and Gary Libbin, provided much-appreciated help in the preparation of the manuscript. As always, my husband encouraged and helped me at every step, for which I am ever grateful.

Adele Berlin

# ABBREVIATIONS

| | |
|---|---|
| AB | Anchor Bible |
| *ABD* | *Anchor Bible Dictionary* |
| *ANET* | *Ancient Near Eastern Texts Relating to the Old Testament.* Edited by J. B. Pritchard. 3d ed. Princeton: Princeton University Press, 1969 |
| *Bib* | *Biblica* |
| *BibInt* | *Biblical Interpretation* |
| BZAW | Beihefte zur Zeitschrift für die alttestamentliche Wissenschaft |
| *CBQ* | *Catholic Biblical Quarterly* |
| *CurTM* | *Currents in Theology and Mission* |
| *DBI* | *Dictionary of Biblical Interpretation* |
| DJD | Discoveries in the Judean Desert |
| FCB | Feminist Companion to the Bible |
| FOTL | Forms of the Old Testament Literature |
| *HAR* | *Hebrew Annual Review* |
| *HALOT* | *Hebrew and Aramaic Lexicon of the Old Testament.* Edited by Ludwig Koehler, et al. Translated and edited by M. E. J. Richardson, et al. 5 vols. Leiden: Brill, 1994–2000 |
| *HeyJ* | *Heythrop Journal* |
| Hillers | Hillers, *Lamentations* (1992) |
| *HTR* | *Harvard Theological Review* |
| *IDBSup* | *Interpreter's Dictionary of the Bible, Supplementary Volume* |
| *JANES* | *Journal of the Ancient Near Eastern Society* |
| *JAOS* | *Journal of the American Oriental Society* |
| *JBL* | *Journal of Biblical Literature* |
| *JCS* | *Journal of Cuneiform Studies* |
| *JNSL* | *Journal of Northwest Semitic Languages* |
| *JQR* | *Jewish Quarterly Review* |
| *JR* | *Journal of Religion* |
| JSJSup | Journal for the Study of Judaism Supplement |
| *JSOT* | *Journal for the Study of the Old Testament* |
| JSOTSup | Journal for the Study of the Old Testament Supplement Series |

| KJV | King James Version |
|---|---|
| LXX | Septuagint |
| MT | Masoretic Text |
| NEB | New English Bible |
| *NIB* | *New Interpreter's Bible* |
| NIV | New International Version |
| NJPS | New Jewish Publication Society |
| NOAB | New Oxford Annotated Bible |
| NRSV | New Revised Standard Version |
| OBT | Overtures to Biblical Theology |
| *OTE* | *Old Testament Essays* |
| OTL | Old Testament Library |
| *OTWSA* | *Ou-Testamentiese Werkgemeenskaf in Suid-Afrika* |
| *PEQ* | *Palestine Exploration Quarterly* |
| Provan | Provan, *Lamentations* |
| *RB* | *Revue biblique* |
| REB | Revised English Bible |
| Renkema | Renkema, *Lamentations* |
| RSV | Revised Standard Version |
| SBLDS | Society of Biblical Literature Dissertation Series |
| SBLEJL | Society of Biblical Literature Early Judaism and Its Literature |
| SBLMS | Society of Biblical Literature Monograph Series |
| *SJOT* | *Scandinavian Journal of the Old Testament* |
| SubBi | Subsidia biblica |
| *TDOT* | *Theological Dictionary of the Old Testament* |
| *UET* | *Ur Excavation Texts* |
| *VT* | *Vetus Testamentum* |
| Westermann | Westermann, *Lamentations* |
| *ZAW* | *Zeitschrift für die alttestamentliche Wissenschaft* |

# BIBLIOGRAPHY

I. *Commentaries and Monographs on Lamentations*

Albrektson, Bertil. *Studies in the Text and Theology of the Book of Lamentations*. Lund: Gleerup, 1963.

Bettan, Israel. *The Five Scrolls: A Commentary on the Song of Songs, Ruth, Lamentations, Ecclesiastes, Esther*. Cincinnati: Union of American Hebrew Congregations, 1950.

Dobbs-Allsopp, F. W. *Lamentations*. Interpretation. Louisville: Westminster John Knox. 2002.

―――. "Lamentations," annotations in *The New Oxford Annotated Bible*, 3d ed. Oxford and New York: Oxford University Press, 2001. Pp. 1167–79 Hebrew Bible.

―――. *Weep, O Daughter of Zion: A Study of the City-Lament Genre in the Hebrew Bible*. Biblica et orientalia 44. Rome: Pontifical Biblical Institute Press, 1993.

Gerstenberger, Erhard S. *Psalms, Part 2, and Lamentations*. FOTL 15. Grand Rapids: Eerdmans, 2001.

Gordis, Robert. *The Song of Songs and Lamentations*. New York: Ktav, 1974.

Gottlieb, Hans. *A Study on the Text of Lamentations*. Translated by John Sturdy. Acta Jutlandica 48. Theology Series 12. Århus: Det Laerde Selskab, 1978.

Gottwald, Norman K. *Studies in the Book of Lamentations*. SBT 1/14. Chicago: Allenson; London: SCM, 1954.

―――. "Lamentations." Pp. 646–51 in *Harper's Bible Commentary*, edited by James L. Mays, et al. San Francisco: Harper & Row, 1988.

Guinan, Michael D. "Lamentations." Pp. 558–62 in *The New Jerome Biblical Commentary*, edited by Raymond E. Brown et al. Englewood Cliffs, N.J.: Prentice-Hall, 1990.

Harrison, R. K. *Jeremiah and Lamentations*. Tyndale Old Testament Commentaries. Downers Grove, Ill.: InterVarsity Press, 1973.

Hillers, Delbert R. *Lamentations*. AB 7A. New York: Doubleday, 1972; revised edition, 1992. (The 1992 edition is cited unless otherwise noted.)

Hunter, Jannie. *Faces of a Lamenting City: The Development and Coherence of the Book of Lamentations.* Beiträge zur Erforschung des Alten Testaments und des antiken Judentums 39. Frankfurt am Main: Peter Lang, 1996.

Kaiser, Otto. "Klagelieder." In Helmer Ringgren and Otto Kaiser, *Das Hohe Lied*/Klagelieder/*Das Buch Esther,* pp. 91–198. 4th ed. Das Alte Testament Deutsch 16/2. Göttingen: Vandenhoeck & Ruprecht, 1992.

Klein, J., ed. "Lamentations" (in Hebrew). *Encyclopedia Olam Hatanakh.* 16A:107–59. Ramat Gan: Revivim, n.d.

Kraus, H.-J. *Klagelieder* (Threni). 3d ed. Biblischer Kommentar zum Alten Testament 20. Neukirchen-Vluyn: Neukirchener Verlag, 1968.

Landy, Francis. "Lamentations." In *The Literary Guide to the Bible,* edited by Robert Alter and Frank Kermode, pp. 329–34. Cambridge, Mass.: Belknap, 1987.

Lee, Nancy C. "The Singers of Lamentations: Cities under Siege, from Ur to Jerusalem to Sarajevo." Ph.D. dissertation, Union Theological Seminary and Presbyterian School of Christian Education. Richmond, Va., May 2000.

Linafeldt, Tod. *Surviving Lamentations: Catastrophe, Lament, and Protest in the Afterlife of a Biblical Book.* Chicago: University of Chicago Press, 2000.

Martin-Achard, Robert, and S. Paul Re'emi. *God's People in Crisis: A Commentary on the Book of Amos. A Commentary on the Book of Lamentations.* International Theological Commentary. Grand Rapids: Eerdmans; Edinburgh: Handsel, 1984.

Moskowitz, Yehiel Zvi. "Lamentations" (in Hebrew). *Five Megillot.* Daʿat Miqra Series. Jerusalem: Mosad Harav Kook, 1990.

O'Connor, Kathleen M. "Lamentations." *NIB* 6:1011–72. Nashville: Abingdon, 2001.

———. "Lamentations." Pp. 178–82 in *The Women's Bible Commentary,* edited by Carol A. Newsom and Sharon H. Ringe. Louisville, Ky.: Westminster/John Knox, 1992. (Expanded edition, 1998, pp. 187–91.)

Pham, Xuan Huong Thi. *Mourning in the Ancient Near East and the Hebrew Bible.* JSOTSup 302. Sheffield: Sheffield Academic Press, 1999.

Provan, Iain W. *Lamentations.* New Century Bible Commentary. Grand Rapids: Eerdmans, 1991.

Renkema, Johan. *Lamentations.* Historical Commentary on the Old Testament. Leuven: Peeters, 1998.

Reyburn, William D. *A Handbook on Lamentations.* New York: United Bible Societies, 1992.

Salters, Robert B. *Jonah and Lamentations.* Old Testament Guides. Sheffield: JSOT Press, 1994.

Westermann, Claus. *Lamentations: Issues and Interpretation.* Translated by Charles Muenchow. Minneapolis: Fortress, 1994. (Translation of *Die Klagelieder: Forschungsgeschichte und Auslegung.* Neukirchen-Vluyn: Neukirchener Verlag, 1990.)

II. *Books and General Monographs*

Ackroyd, Peter. *Exile and Restoration: A Study of Hebrew Thought of the Sixth Century B.C. OTL.* Philadelphia: Westminster, 1968.

Alonso Schökel, Luis. *A Manual of Hebrew Poetics.* SubBi II. Rome: Pontifical Biblical Institute, 1988.

Alter, Robert. *The Art of Biblical Poetry.* New York: Basic Books, 1985.

Anderson, Gary A. *A Time to Mourn, a Time to Dance: The Expression of Grief and Joy in Israelite Religion.* University Park, Pa.: Pennsylvania State University Press, 1991.

Bartlett, John R. *Edom and the Edomites.* JSOTSup 77. Sheffield: Sheffield Academic Press. 1989.

Berlin, Adele. *The Dynamics of Biblical Parallelism.* Bloomington: Indiana University Press, 1985.

Bouzard, Walter C., Jr. *We Have Heard with Our Ears, O God: Sources of the Communal Laments in the Psalms.* SBLDS 159. Atlanta: Scholars Press, 1997.

Brenner, Athalya, ed. *The Feminist Companion to the Latter Prophets.* FCB 1/8. Sheffield: Sheffield Academic Press, 1995.

Buber, Salomon. *Midrasch Echa Rabbati.* Vilna: Romm, 1899.

Cohen, A. *Midrash Rabbah. Lamentations.* London: Soncino, 1939.

Cohen, Mark E. *The Canonical Lamentations of Mesopotamia.* 2 vols. Potomac, Md.: CDL, 1988.

———. *Sumerian Hymnology: The Eršemma.* Cincinnati: Hebrew Union College Press. 1981.

Cooper, Jerrold. *The Curse of Agade.* Baltimore: Johns Hopkins University Press, 1983.

Edelman, Diana Vikander, ed. *You Shall Not Abhor an Edomite for He Is Your Brother: Edom and Seir in History and Tradition.* Society of Biblical Literature Archaeology and Biblical Studies 3. Atlanta: Scholars Press, 1995.

Eph'al, Israel. *Ke'ir neṣurah. Ha-maṣor vegiluyyav ba-mizraḥ ha-qadum* (Siege and Its Ancient Near Eastern Manifestations) [in Hebrew]. Jerusalem: Magnes, 1996.

Ferris, Paul Wayne, Jr. *The Genre of Communal Lament in the Bible and the Ancient Near East.* SBLDS 127. Atlanta: Scholars Press, 1992.

Fisch, Harold. *Poetry with a Purpose.* Bloomington: Indiana University Press, 1988.

Frymer-Kensky, Tikva. *In the Wake of the Goddesses: Women, Culture, and the Biblical Transformation of Pagan Myth.* New York: Free Press, 1992.

Galambush, Julie. *Jerusalem in the Book of Ezekiel: The City as Yahweh's Wife.* SBLDS 130. Atlanta: Scholars Press, 1992.

Gray, G. B. *The Form of Hebrew Poetry.* 1915. Reprint, New York: Ktav, 1972.

Grossberg, Daniel. *Centripetal and Centrifugal Structures in Biblical Poetry.* SBLMS 39. Atlanta: Scholars Press, 1989.

Jahnow, Hedwig. *Das hebräische Leichenlied im Rahmen der Völkerdichtung.* BZAW 125. Giessen: Töpelmann, 1923.

Kartveit, Magnar. "The Virgin Israel and Her Cognates. Hebrew Construct Chains with Internally Applied Metaphors in the Nomen Regens." Unpublished manuscript.

Klein, Ralph. *Israel in Exile. A Theological Interpretation.* OBT. Philadelphia: Fortress, 1979.

Levine, Etan. *The Aramaic Version of Lamentations.* New York: Hermon, 1976.

Michalowski, Piotr. *The Lamentation over the Destruction of Sumer and Ur.* Winona Lake, Ind.: Eisenbrauns, 1989.

Miller, Patrick D. *They Cried to the Lord: The Form and Theology of Biblical Prayer.* Minneapolis: Fortress, 1994.

Mintz, Alan. *Ḥurban: Responses to Catastrophe in Hebrew Literature.* New York: Columbia University Press, 1984.

Neusner, Jacob. *Self-Fulfilling Prophecy: Exile and Return in the History of Judaism.* Boston: Beacon, 1987.

————. *Israel after Calamity: The Book of Lamentations.* Valley Forge, Pa.: Trinity Press International, 1995.

Oded, Bustenay. *Mass Deportations and Deportees in the Neo-Assyrian Empire.* Wiesbaden: Reichert, 1979.

Parpola, Simo, and Kazuko Watanabe. *Neo-Assyrian Treaties and Loyalty Oaths.* State Archives of Assyria 2. Helsinki: Helsinki University Press, 1988.

Ryken, Leland, James C. Wilhoit, and T. Longman III, eds. *Dictionary of Biblical Imagery.* Downer's Grove, Ill.: InterVarsity Press, 1998.

Scott, James M., ed. *Exile: Old Testament, Jewish, and Christian Conceptions.* JSJSup 56. Leiden: Brill, 1997.

Smith, Daniel L. *The Religion of the Landless: The Social Context of the Babylonian Exile.* Bloomington, Ind.: Meyer-Stone Books, 1989.

Sommer, Benjamin. *A Prophet Reads Scripture: Allusion in Isaiah 40–66.* Stanford: Stanford University Press, 1998.

Tinney, Steve. *The Nippur Lament: Royal Rhetoric and Divine Legitimation in the Reign of Išme-Dagon of Isin (1953–1935 B.C.).* Occasional Publications of the Samuel Noah Kramer Fund 16. Philadelphia: University Museum, 1996.

Ussishkin, David. *The Conquest of Lachish by Sennacherib.* Tel Aviv: Tel Aviv University, Institute of Archaeology, 1982.

Waltke, Bruce, and Michael O'Connor. *An Introduction to Biblical Hebrew Syntax.* Winona Lake, Ind.: Eisenbrauns, 1990.

Watson, Wilfred G. E. *Classical Hebrew Poetry.* JSOTSup 26. Sheffield: JSOT Press, 1984.

Weinfeld, Moshe. *Deuteronomy 1–11.* AB 5. New York: Doubleday, 1991.

Werline, Rodney A. *Penitential Prayer in Second Temple Judaism: The Development of a Religious Institution.* SBLEJL 13. Atlanta: Scholars Press, 1998.

Willey, Patricia T. *Remember the Former Things: The Recollection of Previous Texts in Second Isaiah.* SBLDS 161. Atlanta: Scholars Press, 1997.

III. *Articles and Chapters*

Ahuvyah, A. "*ʾykh yšbh bdd hꜥyr rbty ꜥm* (Lam 1:1)" (How lonely sits the city . . . full of people) [in Hebrew]. *Beth Miqra* 24 (1979): 423–25.

Alexander, Philip S. "The Textual Tradition of Targum Lamentations." *Abr-Nahrain* 24 (1986): 1–26.

Artzi, Pinhas. "Mourning in International Relations." Pp. 161–70 in *Death in Mesopotamia,* edited by Bendt Alster. Copenhagen: Akademisk Forlag, 1980.

Barré, Michael L. "Treaties in the ANE." *ABD* 6:653–56.

Barré, Michael L., and John Kselman. "New Exodus, Covenant, and Restoration in Psalm 23." Pp. 97–127 in *The Word of the Lord Shall Go Forth: Essays in Honor of David Noel Freedman,* edited by Carol L. Meyers, and Michael O'Connor. Winona Lake, Ind.: Eisenbrauns, 1983.

Bechtel, Lyn M. "Shame as a Sanction of Social Control in Biblical Israel: Judicial, Political, and Social Shaming." *JSOT* 49 (1991): 47–76.

Berges, Ulrich. "Ich bin der Mann, der Elend sah" (Klgl 3,1); Zionstheologie als Weg aus der Krise." *Biblische Zeitschrift* 44,1 (2000): 1–20.

Bergler, Siegfried. "Threni v—nur ein alphabetisierendes Lied: Versuch einer Deutung." *VT* 27 (1977): 304–20.

Berlin, Adele. Review of *Weep, O Daughter of Zion: A Study of the City-Lament Genre in the Hebrew Bible* by F. W. Dobbs-Allsopp. *JAOS* 115 (1995): 319.

Biddle, Mark. "The Figure of Lady Jerusalem: Identification, Deification, and Personification of Cities in the Ancient Near East." Pp. 173–94 in *Scripture in Context,* vol. 4, *The Biblical Canon in Comparative Perspective,* edited by K. L. Younger et al. Lewiston, N.Y.: Edwin Mellen, 1991.

Brug, John F. "Biblical Acrostics and Their Relationship to Other Ancient Near Eastern Acrostics." Pp. 283–304 in *Scripture in Context,* vol. 3, *The Bible in the Light of Cuneiform Literature,* edited by William W. Hallo et al. Lewiston, N.Y.: Edwin Mellen, 1990.

Brunet, Gilbert. "La cinquième Lamentation." *VT* 33 (1983): 149–70.

Budde, Carl. "Das hebräische Klagelied." *ZAW* 2 (1882): 1–52.

Ceresko, Anthony R. "The ABCs of Wisdom in Psalm XXXIV." *VT* 35 (1985): 99–104.

Cohen, Chayim. "The 'Widowed' City." *JANES* 5 (1973): 75–81.

Cohen, Shaye. "The Destruction from Scripture to Midrash." *Prooftexts* 2 (1982): 18–39.

Cross, Frank M. "Studies in the Structure of Hebrew Verse: The Prosody of Lamentations 1:1–22." Pp. 129–55 in *The Word of the Lord Shall Go Forth: Essays in Honor of David Noel Freedman,* edited by Carol L. Meyers and Michael O'Connor. Winona Lake, Ind.: Eisenbrauns, 1983.

Dahood, Mitchell. "New Readings in Lamentations." *Bib* 59 (1978): 174–97.

Day, Peggy. "The Personification of Cities as Female in the Hebrew Bible: The Thesis of Aloysius Fitzgerald, F.S.C." Pp. 283–302 in *Reading from This Place,* vol. 2, *Social Location and Biblical Interpretation in Global Perspective,* edited by Fernando Segovia and Mary Ann Tolbert, Minneapolis: Fortress, 1995.

De Hoop, Raymond. "Lamentations: The Qinah-Metre Questioned." Pp. 80–104 in *Delimitation Criticism. A New Tool in Biblical Scholarship.* Edited by Marjo C. A. Korpel and Josef M. Oesch. Assen: Van Gorcum, 2000.

Dobbs-Allsopp, F. W. "Darwinism, Genre Theory, and City Laments." *JAOS* 120 (2000): 625–30.

―――. "The Effects of Enjambment in Lamentations (Part 2)." *ZAW* 113 (2001): forthcoming.

―――. "The Enjambing Line in Lamentations: A Taxonomy (Part 1)." *ZAW* 113 (2001): 219–39.

―――. "Lamentations as Lyric." Unpublished manuscript.

―――. "Linguistic Evidence for the Date of Lamentations." *JANES* 26 (1998): 1–36.

―――. "The Syntagma of *bat* Followed by a Geographical Name in the Hebrew Bible: A Reconsideration of Its Meaning and Grammar." *CBQ* 57 (1995): 451–70.

―――. "Tragedy, Tradition, and Theology in the Book of Lamentations." *JSOT* 74 (1997): 29–60.

―――. "Zion's Dark Night of Suffering: A Reading of Lamentations 1." Unpublished manuscript.

Dobbs-Allsopp, F. W., and Tod Linafelt. "The Rape of Zion in Thr 1,10." *ZAW* 113,1 (2001): 77–81.

Dorsey, David A. "Lamentations: Communicating Meaning through Structure." *Evangelical Journal* 6 (1988): 83–90.

Durlesser, James A. "The Book of Lamentations and the Mesopotamian Laments: Experiential or Literary Ties." *Proceedings, Eastern Great Lakes Biblical Society* 3 (1983): 69–81.

Emerton, J. A. "The Meaning of ʾabnê-qōdeš in Lamentations 4:1." *ZAW* 79 (1967): 233–36.

Fitzgerald, Aloysius. "*Btwlt* and *Bt* as Titles for Capital Cities." *CBQ* 37 (1975): 167–83.

―――. "The Mythological Background for the Presentation of Jerusalem as Queen and False Worship as Adultery in the OT." *CBQ* 34 (1972): 403–16.

Follis, Elaine R. "The Holy City as Daughter." Pp. 173–84 in *Directions in Biblical Hebrew Poetry,* edited by Elaine R. Follis, JSOTSup 40. Sheffield: JSOT Press, 1987.

———. "Zion, Daughter of." *ABD* 6:1103.

Fox, Nili. "Clapping Hands as a Gesture of Anguish and Anger in Mesopotamia and in Israel." *JANES* 23 (1995): 49–60.

Freedman, David Noel. "Acrostic Poems in the Hebrew Bible: Alphabetic and Otherwise." *CBQ* 48 (1986): 408–31.

———. "Acrostics and Metrics in Hebrew Poetry." Pp. 51–76, in *Pottery, Poetry, and Prophecy: Studies in Early Hebrew Poetry.* Winona Lake, Ind.: Eisenbrauns, 1980.

Frisch, Amos. "*wᶜnytm* (I Reg 12,7): An Ambiguity and Its Function in the Context." *ZAW* 103 (1991): 415–18.

Frymer-Kensky, Tikva. "Pollution, Purification, and Purgation in Biblical Israel." Pp. 399–414 in *The Word of the Lord Shall Go Forth: Essays in Honor of David Noel Freedman,* edited by Carol L. Meyers and Michael O'Connor. Winona Lake, Ind.: Eisenbrauns, 1983.

Galatzer-Levy, R., and M. Gruber. "What an Affect Means: A Quasi-Experiment about Disgust." *Annual of Psychoanalysis* 20 (1992): 69–92.

Garr, W. Randall. "The Qinah: A Study of Poetic Meter, Syntax and Style." *ZAW* 95 (1983): 54–75.

Goerwitz, Richard L. "What Does the Priestly Source Mean by *prᶜ ʾt hrʾš?*" *JQR* 86 (1996): 377–94.

Goitein, S. D. *Iyyunim bammiqra* (Studies in Scripture) (Tel Aviv: Yavneh, 1957), 248–82 (= "Women as Creators of Biblical Genres," *Prooftexts* 8 [1988]: 1–33).

Gordis, Robert. "The Conclusion of the Book of Lamentations (5:22)." *JBL* 93 (1974): 289–93.

———. "A Note on Lamentations ii 13." *Journal of Theological Studies* 34 (1933): 162–63.

Gordon, Pamela, and Harold C. Washington. "Rape as a Military Metaphor in the Hebrew Bible." Pp. 308–25 in *The Feminist Companion to the Latter Prophets,* edited by A. Brenner. Sheffield: Sheffield Academic Press, 1995.

Gosse, Bernard. "Les 'Confessions' de Jérémie, la vengeance contre Jérusalem à l'image de celle contre Babylone et les nations, et Lamentations 1." *ZAW* 111 (1999): 58–67.

Gottwald, Norman K. "Lamentations." *Interpretation* 9 (1955): 320–38.

Gous, Ig. "Exiles and the Dynamics of Experiences of Loss: The Reaction of Lamentations 2 on the Loss of the Land." *OTE* 6 (1993): 351–63.

———. "Lamentations 5 and the Translation of Verse 22." *OTE* 3 (1990): 287–302.

———. "Mind over Matter: Lamentations 4 in the Light of the Cognitive Sciences." *SJOT* 10 (1996): 69–87.

————. "Psychological Survival Strategies in Lamentations 3 in the Light of Neuro-Linguistic Programming." Pp. 317–41 in *Old Testament Science and Reality,* edited by W. Wessels and E. Scheffler, Pretoria: Verba Vitae, 1992.

————. "A Survey of Research on the Book of Lamentations." *OTE* 5 (1992): 184–205.

Graetz, Naomi. "Jerusalem the Widow." *Shofar* 17/2 (winter 1999): 16–24.

Green, Margaret W. "The Eridu Lament." *JCS* 30 (1978): 127–67.

————. "The Uruk Lament." *JAOS* 104 (1984): 253–79.

Greenberg, Moshe. "The Etymology of *niddah* '(Menstrual) Impurity.'" Pp. 69–77 in *Solving Riddles and Untying Knots: Biblical, Epigraphic, and Semitic Studies in Honor of Jonas C. Greenfield,* edited by Ziony Zevit, et al. Winona Lake, Ind.: Eisenbrauns, 1995.

Greenstein, E. "Qinah 'al hurban 'ir umiqdaš besifrut hayisra'elit ha-qedumah" (The Lament over the Destruction of a City and Temple in Early Israelite Literature) [in Hebrew]. Pp. 88–97 in *Homage to Shmuel: Studies in the World of the Bible,* edited by Z. Talshir, S. Yona, and D. Sivan. Jerusalem: Ben Gurion University of the Negev/Bialik Institute, 2001.

Guest, Deryn. "Hiding Behind the Naked Women in Lamentations: A Recriminative Response." *BibInt* 7 (1999): 413–48.

Gunkel, Hermann. "Klagelieder Jeremiae." Pp. 1049–52 in *Die Religion in Geschichte und Gegenwart.* 2d ed. 3. Tübingen: Mohr (Siebeck), 1929.

Gwaltney, W. C., Jr. "The Biblical Book of Lamentations in the Context of Near Eastern Lament Literature." Pp. 191–211 in *Scripture in Context,* vol. 2, *More Essays on the Comparative Method,* edited by William W. Hallo et al. Winona Lake, Ind.: Eisenbrauns, 1983. Reprinted in *Essential Papers on Israel and the Ancient Near East,* edited by Frederick E. Greenspahn, 242–65. New York: New York University Press, 1991.

————. "Lamentations, Book of." *DBI* 2:44–48.

Hallo, William W. "Lamentations and Prayers in Sumer and Akkad." In *Civilizations of the Ancient Near East,* edited by Jack Sasson, 3:1871–81. New York: Charles Scribner's Sons, 1995.

Heim, Knut M. "The Personification of Jerusalem and the Drama of Her Bereavement in Lamentations." Pp. 129–69 in *Zion, City of Our God,* edited by Richard S. Hess and Gordon J. Wenham. Grand Rapids: Eerdmans, 1999.

Helberg, J. L. "The Incomparable Sorrow of Zion in the Book of Lamentations." Pp. 27–36 in *Studies in Wisdom Literature,* edited by C. W. van Wyk. *OTWSA* 15–16. Potchefstrom: Pro Rege, n.d.

————. "Land in the Book of Lamentations." *ZAW* 102 (1990): 372–85.

Hillers, Delbert R. "History and Poetry in Lamentations." *CurTM* 10 (1983): 155–61.

————. "Lamentations, Book of." *ABD* 4:137–41.

————. "Observations on Syntax and Meter in Lamentations." Pp. 265–70 in *A Light unto My Path: Old Testament Studies in Honor of Jacob M. Myers,* edited by Howard M. Bream et al. Philadelphia: Temple University Press, 1974.

Horowitz, T. *"Sugat ha-qinah ha- ʿivrit ha-qlasit"* (The Genre of the Classical Hebrew Lament) [in Hebrew]. *Shaʿanan* 5 (1999): 39–74.

Hurowitz, Victor A. *"zwllh*=peddlar/tramp/vagabond/beggar. Lamentations i 11 in Light of Akkadian *zilulû."* *VT* 49 (1999): 542–45.

Johnson, Bo. "Form and Message in Lamentations." *ZAW* 97 (1985): 58–73.

Joyce, Paul. "Lamentations and the Grief Process: A Psychological Reading." *BibInt* 1 (1993): 304–20.

————. "Sitting Loose to History: Reading the Book of Lamentations without Primary Reference to Its Original Historical Setting." Pp. 246–62 in *In Search of True Wisdom: Essays in Old Testament Interpretation in Honour of Ronald E. Clements,* edited by Edward Ball, JSOTSup 300. Sheffield: JSOT Press, 1999.

Kaiser, Barbra Bakke. "Poet as Female Impersonator: The Image of Daughter Zion as Speaker in Biblical Poems of Suffering." *JR* 67 (1987): 164–82.

Kartveit, Magnar. "Sions dotter." *Tidsskrift for Teologi og Kirke* 1–2 (2001): 97–112.

Kirschner, Robert. "Apocalyptic and Rabbinic Responses to the Destruction of 70." *HTR* 78 (1985): 27–46.

Klein, Jacob. "The Mesopotamian Weeping Goddess and Bat-Zion in the Book of Lamentations." Unpublished seminar paper, Center for Judaic Studies, University of Pennsylvania. September 24, 1997.

Knibb, Michael A. "The Exile in the Literature of the Intertestamental Period." *HeyJ* 17 (1976): 253–72.

Kramer, Samuel N. "The Weeping Goddess: Sumerian Prototypes of the Mater Dolorosa." *Biblical Archaeologist* 46 (1983): 69–80.

Krašovec, Jože. "The Source of Hope in the Book of Lamentations." *VT* 42 (1992): 223–33.

Lachs, Samuel T. "The Date of Lamentations V." *JQR* 57 (1966–67): 46–56.

Lanahan, William F. "The Speaking Voice in the Book of Lamentations." *JBL* 93 (1974): 41–49.

Levine, Baruch. "Silence, Sound, and the Phenomenology of Mourning in Biblical Israel." *JANES* 22 (1993): 89–106.

Linafeldt, Tod. "Margins of Lamentations." Pp. 219–32 in *Reading Bibles, Writing Bodies: Identity and the Book,* edited by Timothy K. Beal and David M. Gunn. London: Routledge, 1997.

————. "Surviving Lamentations." *Horizons in Biblical Theology* 17 (1995): 45–61.

Magdalene, F. Rachel. "Ancient Near Eastern Treaty-Curses and the Ultimate Texts of Terror: A Study of the Language of Divine Sexual Abuse in the

Prophetic Corpus." Pp. 326–53 in *The Feminist Companion to the Latter Prophets*, edited by A. Brenner.

Marcus, David. "Non-recurring Doublets in the Book of Lamentations." *HAR* 10 (1986): 177–95.

McDaniel, Thomas F. "Philological Studies in Lamentations, I." *Bib* 49 (1968): 27–53.

———. "Philological Studies in Lamentations, II." *Bib* 49 (1968): 199–220.

———. "The Alleged Sumerian Influence upon Lamentations." *VT* 18 (1968): 198–209.

Mintz, Alan. "The Rhetoric of Lamentations and the Representation of Catastrophe." *Prooftexts* 2 (1982): 1–17.

Moore, Michael S. "Human Suffering in Lamentations." *RB* 90 (1983): 534–55.

Moran, William L. "The Ancient Near Eastern Background of the Love of God in Deuteronomy." *CBQ* 25 (1963): 77–87.

Newsom, Carol. "Response to Norman K. Gottwald, 'Social Class and Ideology in Isaiah 40–55: An Eagletonian Reading.'" *Semeia* 59 (1992): 73–78.

Oded, Bustanay. "Judah and the Exile." Pp. 435–88 in *Israelite and Judaean History*, edited by John H. Hayes and J. M. Miller. OTL. Philadelphia: Westminster, 1977.

Olyan, Saul M. "Honor, Shame, and Covenant Relations in Ancient Israel." *JBL* 115 (1996): 201–18.

Owens, Pamela Jean. "Personification and Suffering in Lamentations 3." *Austin Seminary Bulletin: Faculty Edition* 105 (1990): 75–90.

Provan, Iain W. "Feasts, Booths and Gardens (Thr 2,6a)." *ZAW* 102 (1990): 254–55.

———. "Past, Present and Future in Lamentations 3:52–66: The Case for a Precative Perfect Re-examined." *VT* 41 (1991): 164–75.

———. "Reading Texts against an Historical Background: The Case of Lamentations 1." *SJOT* 1 (1990): 130–43.

Renkema, Johan. "Does Hebrew *ytwm* Really Mean 'Fatherless'?" *VT* 45 (1995): 119–22.

———. "The Literary Structure of Lamentations (I–IV)." Pp. 294–396 in *The Structural Analysis of Biblical and Canaanite Poetry*, edited by Willem van der Meer and Johannes C. de Moor. JSOTSup 74. Sheffield: JSOT Press, 1988.

———. "The Meaning of the Parallel Acrostics in Lamentations." *VT* 45 (1995): 379–83.

Rosenfeld, A. "Aqrostikhon be-ʾekhah pereq 5" (An Acrostic in Lamentations 5) [in Hebrew]. *Sinai* 110 (5752): 96.

Ruppert, Lothar. "Klagelieder in Israel und Babylonien: Verschiedene Deutungen der Gewalt." Pp. 111–58 in *Gewalt und Gewaltlosigkeit im Alten Testament*, edited by Norbert Lohfink. Freiburg: Herder, 1983.

Salters, R. "Lamentations 1:3: Light from the History of Exegesis." Pp. 73–89 in *A Word in Season: Essays in Honour of William McKane,* edited by James D. Martin and Philip M. Davies. JSOTSup 42. Sheffield: JSOT Press, 1986.

———. "Searching for Pattern in Lamentations." *OTE* 11 (1998): 93–104.

———. "Structure and Implication in Lamentations 1?" *SJOT* 14 (2000): 293–300.

———. "Using Rashi, Ibn Ezra and Joseph Kara on Lamentations." *JNSL* 25 (1999): 201–13.

Saebø, Magne. "Who Is 'the Man' in Lamentations 3? A Fresh Approach to the Interpretation of the Book of Lamentations." Pp. 294–306 in *Understanding Poets and Prophets: Essays in Honour of George Wishart Anderson.* Edited by A. Graeme Auld. Sheffield: JSOT Press, 1993.

Schramm, Gene M. "Poetic Patterning in Biblical Hebrew." Pp. 167–91 in *Michigan Oriental Studies in Honor of G. G. Cameron,* edited by L. Orlin et al. Ann Arbor: University of Michigan Press, 1976.

Seow, Choon-Leong. "A Textual Note on Lamentations 1:20." *CBQ* 47 (1985): 416–19.

Shea, William H. "Qinah Meter and Strophic Structure in Psalm 137." *HAR* 8 (1984): 199–214.

———. "The *qinah* Structure of the Book of Lamentations." *Bib* 60 (1979): 103–7.

Smith, Mark S. "The Heart and Innards in Israelite Emotional Expressions: Notes from Anthropology and Psychobiology." *JBL* 117 (1998): 427–36.

Smith-Christopher, D. L. "Reassessing the Historical and Sociological Impact of the Babylonian Exile (598/587–539 BCE)." Pp. 7–36 in *Exile: Old Testament, Jewish, and Christian Conceptions,* edited by J. Scott. Leiden: Brill, 1997.

Soll, Will. "Acrostic." *ABD* 1:58–60.

———. "Babylonian and Biblical Acrostics." *Bib* 69 (1988): 305–23.

Stinespring, William R. "No Daughter of Zion." *Encounter* 26 (1965): 133–41.

———. "Zion, Daughter of." *IDBSup,* 985.

Thompson, J. A. "Israel's 'Lovers.'" *VT* 27 (1977): 475–81.

Tigay, Jeffrey. "Lamentations, Book of." *Encyclopaedia Judaica* 10:1368–75. Jerusalem: Keter, 1971.

Vanstiphout, Herman L. J. "The Death of an Era: The Great Mortality in the Sumerian City Laments." Pp. 83–89 in *Death in Mesopotamia,* edited by Bendt Alster. Copenhagen: Akademisk Forlag, 1980.

Watson, Wilfred G. E. "The Unnoticed Word Pair 'eye(s)' // 'heart.'" *ZAW* 101 (1989): 398–409.

Weissblueth, S. "*Mipî ʿelyôn lōʾ tēṣēʾ hārāʿôt wehaṭṭôb*" (It Is Not from the Mouth of the Most High That Good and Evil Comes [Lam 3:38]) [in Hebrew]. *Beth Miqra* 32 (1986–87): 64–67.

Westermann, Claus. "Struktur und Geschichte der Klage im Alten Testament."

*ZAW* 88 (1954): 44–80. (= *Praise and Lament in the Psalms,* 165–213.)

Westhuizen, J. P. van der. "Literary Devices as an Aid to Exegesis." Pp. 149–61 in *Aspects of the Exegetical Process,* edited by W. C. van Wyk. *OTWSA* (1977–1978) 20–21. Pretoria: University of Pretoria and University of the Orange Free State.

Williamson, H. G. M. "Laments at the Destroyed Temple: Excavating the Biblical Text Reveals Ancient Jewish Prayers." *Bible Review* 6 (1990): 12–17, 44.

# INTRODUCTION

The book of Lamentations is a collection of poetic laments for the destruction of the temple and the city of Jerusalem. This was an event without precedent in the history of Israel, and it would become a turning point in Jewish religious development. The destruction of Jerusalem is the event in which the long narrative from Genesis through Kings culminates, about which the prophets warned, and which leaves its mark on all subsequent literature of the Bible. But Lamentations does not look forward and does not look back, does not dwell on what went before or will come after—its gaze is fixed directly on the event itself. In the words of Francis Landy, "it marks, with untempered immediacy, the focal calamity of the Bible, the destruction of Jerusalem in 586 BCE."[1] Lamentations is an expression of the suffering and grief associated with the calamity of destruction, but even more, it is a memorialization of that suffering and grief. It eternalizes the catastrophic moment and its aftermath, freezing it in time, probing it from various perspectives, and preserving it forever.

Although the book is set against the background of a known historical event, the particular historical references to which certain few verses seem to point are obscure. Like much of biblical poetry, Lamentations tends to be nonspecific about names, dates, and places. While Judah and Jerusalem are invoked by name, Babylonia is never mentioned. Zedekiah is probably meant in 4:20 but his name does not appear, nor does the name of Jehoiachin, Nebuchadnezzar, or any other historically noteworthy individual. If we did not know the history of the fall of Judah from other sources, we would have only the vaguest notion of when and how it happened. As Delbert Hillers noted, "such 'history' as we have in Lamentations is not told with an eye to the unique, particular, unrepeatable, contingent circumstances; it is experienced and narrated in conformity to certain pre-existing literary and religious patterns."[2] Hillers was not implying that the event was not unique, or that the biblical authors thought it was not unique; on the contrary, the destruction of Jerusalem stands alone in

---

1. F. Landy, "Lamentations," 329.
2. D. Hillers, "History and Poetry in Lamentations," *CurTM* 10 (1983): 160.

the Bible in its significance and its singularity. But the poetic representation of this focal event is conveyed by means of conventional literary motifs and against the background of Israelite religious concepts.

## 1. The Poetry of Lamentations

Poetry is less transparent than prose and more difficult to understand. Its terseness, its dearth of connecting particles and explanatory phrases, its metaphors, and its intense and imaginative use of language all make interpreting poetry a challenge. For the most part, the poetry of Lamentations is like other biblical poetry, whose formal features are well documented and need not be discussed here.[3] Biblical poetry achieves its "poeticalness" by virtue of its high density of word and sound repetition and its extensive imagery, held together by a pervasive use of parallelism, the main organizing feature of the poetry.

*Qinah meter.* The hallmark of biblical poetry is the parallelism in adjacent lines, a device that has a powerful effect on the movement and meaning of the poem. In most biblical poetry, parallel lines tend to be of similar length, and that is the source of the rhythm. (I use the term *rhythm* because I do not think there is actual meter, in any countable sense, in biblical poetry.) In Lamentations, many sets of lines are of unequal length, producing a rhythm usually called *qinah* meter (those who speak in terms of meter often describe it as 3:2 in terms of accented syllables, and those who speak in syntactic terms say that the first line is an independent thought and the second line is dependent on it).[4] The effect of *qinah* meter, that is, the rhythm of dirges, is sometimes said to be more solemn than the effect of more evenly balanced rhythms, and that may be

---

3. For descriptions of biblical poetry see L. Alonso Schökel, *A Manual of Hebrew Poetic,* SubB: 11 (Rome: Pontifical Biblical Institute, 1988); R. Alter, *The Art of Biblical Poetry* (New York: Basic Books, 1985); A. Berlin, "Introduction to Hebrew Poetry," *NIB* 4:301–15; and W. G. E. Watson, *Classical Hebrew Poetry,* JSOTSup 26 (Sheffield: JSOT Press, 1984). For studies of the poetic aspects of Lamentations see F. W. Dobbs-Allsopp, "The Enjambing Line in Lamentations" (unpublished); G. B. Gray, *The Form of Hebrew Poetry* (1915; repr. New York: Ktav, 1972); D. Grossberg, *Centripetal and Centrifugal Structures in Biblical Poetry,* SBLMS 39 (Atlanta: Scholars Press, 1989); J. Renkema, "The Literary Structure of Lamentations," in *The Structural Analysis of Biblical and Canaanite Poetry,* ed. W. van der Meer and J. C. de Moor, JSOTSup 74 (Sheffield: JSOT Press, 1988), 294–396; G. M. Schramm, "Poetic Patterning in Biblical Hebrew," in *Michigan Oriental Studies in Honor of G. G. Cameron,* ed. L. Orlin et al. (Ann Arbor: University of Michigan Press, 1976), 167–91.

4. See C. Budde, "Das hebräische Klagelied"; and R. Garr, "The Qinah: A Study of Poetic Meter, Syntax and Style," *ZAW* 95 (1983): 54–75. W. H. Shea, "The *qinah* Structure," suggests that the entire book is structured on the *qinah* pattern, with the first unit being three chapters, followed by a shorter unit of two chapters. But this is a rather far-fetched extension of what is usually meant by the *qinah* pattern. For a recent critique of the concept of *qinah* meter see Raymond de Hoop, "Lamentations: The Qinah-Metre Questioned."

so; but it should be noted that *qinah* meter is used in some nonlament poems and not all dirges are in *qinah* meter (see Hillers, 18–19).

*Other aural features.* Rhythm is one part of the aural dimension of poetry, a genre that is essentially aural (meant to be heard). Other aural effects include the repetition of words and the use of key words, the patterning of words and sounds, and plays on words and on sounds. Although occurring frequently in the Hebrew, these aural features are not readily represented in English. The classic places where many English translations try to capture the sound-play are 2:5 and 3:47. These translations use alliteration, "mourning and moaning" for *taʾăniyyâ waʾăniyyâ* (2:5), although the Hebrew trope is actually the reverse of the English one. The English alliterates the first letter of each word, whereas the Hebrew has "rhyme" in all but the first letter. In the Hebrew, *paḥad wāpaḥat* (3:47) involves the repetition of the sound of all the consonants, not just the first, as in the English "panic and pitfall." Alliteration (the repetition of initial identical consonants), a common trope in English poetry, is an incidental feature of Hebrew poetry. Sound repetition in Hebrew generally involves several consonants, not necessarily the first ones and not always identical ones. So when English translations use alliteration to convey the sound-play of the Hebrew words, they are "translating" one poetic trope into another.

*Linguistic style.* The linguistic style of Lamentations does not appear to differ from other biblical poetry of its period and genre, although its poems are more vivid than other laments. Part of the book's linguistic interest stems from its use of rare denominative verbs in place of their more common nouns. Examples are *ngh* (1:4, 5) instead of *yāgôn,* and *yāʿîb* (2:1) for *tôʿēbâ* (according to some interpretations). Another technique is the use of homonyms, the same word with different meanings in close proximity: *ʿôlal* (2:20) meaning "to do"/"little child"; *môʿēd* (2:6) for "tabernacle" and "festival"; *rabbātî* (1:1) in the sense of "thronged with" and "noble."

*Grammatical tense* is a particularly vexing feature to render in English, in part because past (perfect) and future (imperfect) often alternate in poetry. We do not always know when the poet of Lamentations was speaking of past suffering or of suffering yet to come. In many instances, both past and future signify the ongoing present. The suffering in Lamentations is timeless, and the expression of this timelessness seems to have been one of the poet's goals.

*Imagery,* a hallmark of poetry, is ubiquitous in Lamentations. No sooner is one image conjured up than it fades into another. Metaphors are not always easy to grasp and may set in motion a chain of associations that cannot be easily articulated. Metaphors come in different sizes. Some are local metaphors, expressions of a few words, like "her princes have become like stags" (1:6). Others are global, involving broad religious concepts like the husband-wife metaphor for God's relationship with Israel. In the past, most studies of biblical poetry have slighted metaphor in favor of formal poetic devices like meter and parallelism, and most commentaries pay minimal attention to explaining the imagery. Since much of the meaning of the poetry resides in its metaphors, this commentary devotes considerable effort to unpacking them.

*Hendiadys.* A common figure of speech is hendiadys, the expression of an idea by two independent words connected by the conjunctive particle *waw*, "and," instead of using an independent word and its modifier. The identification of a hendiadys is largely a judgment call. The following are examples of possible hendiadys: 1:7 (cf. 3:19): "misery and trouble" or "miserable trouble"; 2:5: "mourning and moaning" or "mournful moaning"; 2:9: "wrecked and shattered" or "smashed into bits" (NJPS); 3:8: "cry out and plead" or "cry out pleadingly"; 3:18: "my future and my hope" or "my hope for the future"; 3:19: "bitterness and wormwood" or "bitter wormwood"; 3:26: "wait and be still" or "wait patiently" (NJPS); 3:42: " we have sinned and rebelled" or "we have sinned by rebelling"; 3:45: "filth and refuse" or "disgusting filth"; 3:56: "my groan, my cry" or, as I have rendered, "my plea for relief" (so NIV, even though the conjunctive "and" is lacking and so this may not be a true hendiadys); 4:12: "the enemy and the foe" or "the hostile foe"; 4:21: "rejoice and be glad" or "rejoice happily."

*Alphabetic acrostics.* The first four chapters of Lamentations are structured as alphabetic acrostics.[5] The reversal of the letters *pê* and *ᶜayin* in chapters 2, 3, and 4 reflects an alternative order of the alphabet, also found in inscriptions dating from several centuries before 586 B.C.E. at Kuntillet ᶜAjrud and ᶜIzbet Ṣarṭah. Acrostics are not unique to our book, and those who have studied them have seen them as mnemonic devices, aesthetic devices, or a way to express completeness (everything from A to Z), especially if it could never all really be expressed.[6] It is perhaps a sublime literary touch that the poems of this book, which express the inexpressible, use such a formal and rigid style, whose con-

5. On acrostics see J. Brug, "Biblical Acrostics and Their Relationship to Other Ancient Near Eastern Acrostics," in *Scripture in Context,* vol. 3: *The Bible in the Light of Cuneiform Literature,* ed. W. Hallo et al. (Lewiston, N.Y.: Edwin Mellen, 1990), 283–304; A. Ceresko, "The ABCs of Wisdom in Psalm XXXIV," *VT* 35 (1985): 99–104; D. N. Freedman, "Acrostics and Metrics in Hebrew Poetry," in *Pottery, Poetry, and Prophecy* (Winona Lake, Ind.: Eisenbrauns, 1980), 51–76; idem, "Acrostic Poems in the Hebrew Bible: Alphabetic and Otherwise," *CBQ* 48 (1986): 408–31; N. Gottwald, *Studies in the Book of Lamentations,* 23–32; J. Renkema, "The Meaning of the Parallel Acrostics in Lamentations," *VT* 45 (1995): 379–83 (he suggests that there is a connection between all the *ᵓalef* verses in each chapter, the *bêt* verses, etc.); W. Soll, "Acrostic," *ABD* 1:58–60; idem, "Babylonian and Biblical Acrostics," *Bib* 69 (1988): 305–23.

6. The midrash explains the acrostics in the following way: "Why is the Book of Lamentations composed as an alphabetic acrostic? R. Judah, R. Nehemiah, and the Rabbis suggest answers. R. Judah said: Because it is written, *Yea, all Israel have transgressed Thy law* (Dan. ix, 11), which is written [with all the letters] from *alef* to *taw*; therefore is this Book composed as an alphabetical acrostic, one corresponding to the other" (A. Cohen, *Midrash Rabbah, Lamentations* [London: Soncino, 1939], 87).

trolling structural device is the very letters that signify and give shape to language. The world order of Lamentations has been disrupted; no order exists any longer in the real world. But as if to counteract this chaos, the poet has constructed his own linguistic order that he marks out graphically for us by the orderly progression of the letters of the alphabet.[7]

*Parataxis and cohesion.* All poetry is paratactic; the connection between lines is implicit but unmarked, or marked ambiguously. At times in Lamentations there is no copula between lines, and at other times the multivalent copula *wāw* is present. The *wāw* sometimes occurs where we expect it and sometimes not; moreover, sometimes it is translatable and sometimes not.[8] The acrostical structure of four of the chapters exaggerates the sense that each verse stands as a unit unto itself—a complete thought marked by its letter of the alphabet. Yet at the same time, the acrostic binds the chapter into a whole, a complete alphabet.

A major part of understanding a poem is discerning the relationships between and among its verses, between the parts that make up the whole. Parataxis makes determining the relationships difficult, because paratactic lines resist connection.[9] Parataxis acts like a magnet that repels adjacent lines or verses. Other features, however, like parallelism and repetition, work like an attracting magnet to promote the cohesion of the parts of the text. The result is an exegetical pushing and pulling as the interpeter seeks to understand the set of relationships operating within the text. At different times in its history, exegetical trends have encouraged either the paratactic approach or the cohesive approach. Traditional exegesis has concentrated on individual verses, not on the poem as a whole, but nowadays exegetes are more concerned with a view of the whole pericope or chapter, or even book. Toward that end, many commentaries divide the chapters into subsections, usually based on the contents or on a change in the speaking voice, and, for the convenience of the reader, I have done likewise. But these subdivisions are artificial constructs of the exegete; moreover, they are arbitrary in that there is always something driving the poem forward, beyond the subdivision. Often, the formal boundaries of the verses or the parallelisms are in tension with the onward movement of the thought, but this is a productive tension, reminding us that poetry tends not to convey its contents in a linear progression.[10]

---

7. Compare Landy, "Lamentations," 333: "The acrostic is a sign of language—the system of signs—in which all the letters of the alphabet cooperate to generate meaning. Beyond this it is a sign of language as play, free of signification, of the multiple word games that permeate Hebrew poetry."

8. See R. Steiner, "Does the Biblical Hebrew Conjunction -ו Have Many Meanings, One Meaning, or No Meaning at All?" *JBL* 119 (2000): 249–67.

9. Cf. Landy, "Lamentations," 330.

10. See Grossberg, *Centripetal and Centrifugal Structures*, 83–104.

The relationship among the five chapters of the book has also been a subject of study. Some critics have found formal correspondences between parts of a chapter[11] or between one chapter and another,[12] but these seem to me to be at best coincidental and at worst a contrivance of the critic. In any case, they have not been widely accepted. Each chapter has a distinctive tone and set of images, although they all share certain common, even stereotypical, themes related to destruction, and four of the chapters are structured as acrostics. (Renkema has described many of the structural and thematic similarities.) Were the five chapters designed from the outset as parts of the book as it stands now? Or were the chapters originally independent poems, later collected into a book? It seems more likely that the book is a collection of originally separate poems, brought together because they share the same theme of lamenting Jerusalem. This collection of lamentations is not unlike the collections of psalms, proverbs, and love songs that constitute the books of Psalms, Proverbs, and Song of Songs, respectively. If so, the order of the chapters may not have any special significance, or may follow a principle that eludes us. On the other hand, as will become clear below, to conceive of the five chapters as a coherent whole conveying a multifaceted picture of the destruction is a useful exegetical strategy.

*The speaking voices.* It has become customary to identify the speaking voices in the poems—the voice of the feminine Jerusalem, individual male voices, and communal voices.[13] This is part and parcel of a literary understanding of the poems and the perspectives they express. That different exegetes find different speakers is a sign of the variety of interpretations that are possible, or a sign that such identification is as much a product of the interpreter as a feature of the text. Whatever speakers we identify, it is important not to mistake them for authors, witnesses, or historical persons. The voice in chapter 3 may sound like a survivor's, but there is no reason to conclude that an actual survivor wrote the chapter. We must distinguish between the real author and the implied author (the voice that seems to be speaking or writing a particular piece). In Lamentations even the implied author is not easy to identify. I imag-

11. Moskowitz finds a correlation in chaps. 1 and 2 in which elements in v. 1 are picked up in v. 22, elements in v. 2 occur in v. 21, and so forth. This is a loose form of the device called in Hebrew *atbash.*

12. Renkema sees a relationship between the *'alef* verses of chaps. 1–4 and the first verse of chap. 5, the *bet* verses, and so forth. Schramm, "Poetic Patterning," sees a sonnet form, since the first three chapters have 132 lines each, for a total of 396, and the last two have a total of 132.

13. See especially W. Lanahan, "The Speaking Voice in the Book of Lamentations," *JBL* 93 (1974): 41–49; and B. Kaiser, "Poet as Female Impersonator: The Image of Daughter Zion as Speaker in Biblical Poems of Suffering," *JR* 67 (1987): 164–82. The most highly developed analysis of the speakers is K. Heim, "The Personification of Jerusalem and the Drama of Her Bereavement in Lamentations." Heim sees the entire book as a dramatic dialogue of different personae. The drama is a literary artifice that reflects the real-life drama of bereavement.

ine the chapters as spoken by different voices who stand in different locations in reference to the destruction. This interpretive strategy affords me a focal point for interpreting the individual chapters and provides, in turn, a coherent way to think of the combination of the chapters. The speaking voices appear in five different locations or contexts that represent five different aspects of the destruction.

Each chapter presents the destruction from a different perspective. Chapter 1 focuses on Jerusalem, the destroyed city, pictured in her mourning, her shame, and her desolation. The tone is one of despair, depression, degradation, shame, and guilt. The destruction is complete and the reader stands among the ruins. Chapter 2 takes the reader back to the moment of destruction, with all its physical and theological force. The picture is full of anger and fury—God's anger at the city and the poet's anger at God. The chapter focuses on God, the perpetrator of the destruction. The anger of God overshadows the guilt of Jerusalem. Chapter 3 portrays the process of exile, with its alternating moods of despair and hope. The speaker is a lone male, a Joblike figure trying to come to terms with what has happened. His view is personal but at the same time representative of the people. Chapter 4 focuses on the people, reliving the siege and the suffering that accompanied it—the toll it took on the inhabitants of the city. The chapter paints a picture of utter degradation. Chapter 5 is the prayer of the Judean remnant, weakened and impoverished, deprived of king and temple, pleading with God not to abandon them forever, hoping that the former relationship between God and Israel will be renewed.

## 2.  Gender and Suffering

Lamentations is gendered in an essential way in respect to suffering, the central theme of the book. Men and women suffer differently, or, to put it in literary terms, the images for male and female suffering are different.[14] Two sets of images symbolize female suffering: wife and mother, the two major roles that women had in Israelite society and the roles that are lost as a result of the destruction. The wife has lost her husband, and the mother has lost her children.

The wife image often has a sexual connotation, but at times it is devoid of that connotation, especially when the wife is a widow (widows do not engage in sexual activities).[15] The first image in the book is the city as widow (1:1), and later we see the widowed mothers (5:3). The widow, along with the orphan, represents the unprotected, the disadvantaged, so the use of the widow image

---

14. For a critique of the concentration on the male sufferer and the lack of attention to the female sufferer see Linafelt, *Surviving Lamentations*, 1–18.

15. The assumption that widows are chaste is used to good advantage in the story of Judith, for one does not expect a widow to be seductive.

evokes a sociological status, not a sexual one. Moreover, the widow, unlike the other disadvantaged groups in society, has the added connotation of being alone. The widow image, therefore, evokes a double measure of pity, once as a nongendered member of an unprotected group and a second time as an icon of female sadness and vulnerability, a woman deprived of her husband and hence of her place in society, a bereaved and lonely woman. That certainly is the intent of 1:1, and in this connection it is noteworthy that the city is widowed and not "divorced," as she is in some prophetic passages where blame rather than pity is the intended reaction (e.g., Hos 2:4).

The image of wife lends itself to the sexual connotation of unfaithfulness (a widow cannot be unfaithful). The adulterous wife is a common prophetic metaphor for the idolatry of Israel, and chapter 1 makes skillful use of this metaphor. Jerusalem is personified as an unfaithful wife who has taken lovers. For this sexual misconduct, she is sexually shamed by having her nakedness revealed (a measure-for-measure punishment). Unlike the widowed city, the image of the unfaithful city *does* evoke blame, for adultery is a heinous crime, a capital offense. Along with the blame comes repugnance and disgust,[16] because the imagery is about indecency as well as immorality. Since the purpose of Lamentations 1 is not mainly to assess blame, the poem mixes in images of rape, abuse, and abandonment, which shade the blame with horror, pity, and regret. These sexual images are really part of the paradigm of impurity (see below), and as such they have a set of connotations that go beyond the merely sexual; but the vivid sexuality of them cannot be denied, and is extraordinarily effective. Jerusalem, personified as a woman, suffers as only a woman can suffer. For the most part, this highly charged sexual imagery is confined to chapter 1, but the negative sexual image of a woman exposing herself is also applied to Edom, who will, when her turns comes, exchange places with Zion (4:17).

Some feminist readers have been sharply critical of the use of female sexual imagery in the prophetic books and in Lamentations. The more radical among them wish these passages could be excised from the Bible because, they claim, such language and imagery, sexist and violent as it is, denigrates women and even promotes the abuse of women.[17] The imagery is certainly sexual, violent, and degrading, and it is largely thanks to feminist interpretation that we have become sensitive to this fact.[18] But I cannot agree that these images are harm-

---

16. Disgust, as a psychoanalytic term, is associated with bodily sensations and images, including sexual ones. See R. Galatzer-Levy and M. Gruber, "What an Affect Means: A Quasi-Experiment about Disgust,"*Annual of Psychoanalysis* 20 (1992): 69–92.

17. Especially D. Guest, "Hiding behind the Naked Women"; see also N. Graetz, "Jerusalem the Widow"; and K. O'Connor, *Women's Bible Commentary*, 179. For parts of my discussion on this topic I have benefited from the research paper of Helen Leneman.

18. See, however, Alan Mintz, who recognized the presence of rape imagery ("The Rhetoric of Lamentations," 4; *Hurban*, 25).

ful to women in the real world or that they promote sexual abuse or denigrate women. The author personifies Jerusalem as a woman because this is commonplace in his world of thought. He chooses particular female images precisely because they are shocking and do not represent normative behavior. The imagery is meant to evoke a strong feeling of horror and outrage, immorality and shame, suffering and pity, because this mixture of reactions is a crucial part of the poet's message. If readers feel the self-blame and self-pity, the sympathy and disgust, and the violence and sense of being violated, then the poet has succeeded. Feminists are to be commended for showing us the depth of these images, but they ought not then wish them away, for they are the heart of the poetry. They are no more "pornographic" than the images of general human suffering that suffuse the book and are every bit as necessary for the message. The poet wants to show that Jerusalem is in the most horrendous condition conceivable, and for that he chooses the image of an abused woman. Surely this does not denigrate women. If anything, it says that there is no suffering worse than that of an abused woman. Even the most unfaithful of women, says the poet, should not have to suffer the sexual abuse and degradation that Jerusalem suffered.

The other female image in Lamentations, the maternal image, is used for the real mothers of Judah, who lose their maternal status by virtue of the fact that they cannot care for and nourish their children. Indeed, they become the antithesis of mothers—cannibals who eat their children instead of feeding them (2:12, 20; 4:10). For women, this is the worst suffering imaginable. While cannibalism is a conventional image associated with war (see comment on 2:20), it is effective nonetheless. There is no other way that mothers, as mothers, are said to suffer, although they are included in the general suffering and degradation of the siege (e.g., 4:5). Feminist interpreters have concentrated on the sexual imagery but have ignored the maternal imagery, which, in terms of the theme of human suffering, is more poignant and more important.

The men suffer in a typically masculine way—they lose power and physical prowess. No longer in control of their private affairs or the affairs of state, weakened from hunger and disease, they are vanquished by the enemy. Chapter 3 is especially vivid in this regard, with its military imagery and its physical brutality. Men also suffer a loss of their role as protector of the family. Chapter 5 complains that families are bereft of their head-of-household and their ancestral landholdings. Thus suffering is expressed, in large measure, in heavily gendered terms, paralleling the typical roles in society for men and women.

The poet's purpose in dwelling on suffering is, in my view, to make God see the suffering of his people, with the hope that this will provoke a response from him. The poet wants to make God participate in the national experience. The suffering that is put before God is the suffering of all the people, as a whole and in its component parts. It is the suffering of the men and women, the old and young, the rich and poor, the elite and common. Suffering in this book knows no limits of gender or age or class, for the hierarchy in which these distinctions are operative has been destroyed. I do not mean to say that the book sees the end of this hierarchy as an ideal or a goal. On the contrary, the book hopes for its return, for that would be a return to normal. The picture we are shown in these poems is one in which society has broken down completely: the rich are destitute; the leaders are not respected; priests, prophets, and elders have lost their roles in society; ordinary men and women cannot function as they should; and God is silent. This utter meltdown of life as it should be is what the poet is conveying, and what he wants God to notice.

### Excursus 1
### *Bat-ṣiyyôn*, the Personified Zion

Throughout Lamentations, and especially in chapter 1, Jerusalem is personified as a woman. One way that this personification is marked, indeed emphasized, is by the use of the term *bat* in the expression *bat-ṣiyyôn, bĕtûlat bat ṣiyyôn*, and the like. These expressions, akin to epithets, occur twenty times in Lamentations and sixteen times in Jeremiah, out of a total of about forty-five times in the Hebrew Bible. While the term predates the seventh and sixth centuries (Micah and Isaiah use it), its use seems to have peaked in sixth-century texts and may be a hallmark of Lamentations and its traditionally ascribed author, Jeremiah.[19] I mention only in passing the question of the origin of these expressions in the ancient Near Eastern idea of city goddesses, a topic that deserves careful review. Here I will comment briefly on the grammar and meaning of the expressions as we find them in Lamentations and elsewhere in the Bible.

### *The Grammar of Bat X*

*Bat X* is generally understood as an appositional genitive, or a genitive of association. That means that *X* belongs to the class of *bat*.[20] While one could translate "Daughter of Zion" (in the sense of "city of Baltimore," as Dobbs-Allsopp remarks), this translation can be misleading, since it is not Zion's daughter who is being addressed (Zion has no daughter) but Zion herself, who is classified as a "daughter." Another way to put it is to say that the two words should be viewed as being in apposition. "Daughter Zion" is therefore the preferable (literal) translation.[21] Aloysius Fitzgerald, who suggested that *bat* and *bĕtûlat* serve as titles for cities, at first rejected altogether the notion of a genitive construction and took the two nouns as being in apposition; in a second article, he

---

19. See Hillers, 30–31.

20. Waltke and O'Connor, *Biblical Hebrew Syntax*, 153, 226; for other references supporting this position see Dobbs-Allsopp, "The Syntagma of *bat*," 452 n. 2. Follis ("The Holy City as Daughter") takes *bat* literally as "daughter" because she thinks there is a concept of the city as the daughter of the god, but this thesis has little merit.

21. Stinespring argued this point strongly in "No Daughter of Zion," *Encounter* 26 (1965): 133–41; "Zion, daughter of," *IDBSup*, 985.

softened his position, admitting that the appositional genitive does exist in Hebrew and that *bat-ṣiyyôn* and *bĕtûlat bat-ṣiyyôn* may be examples of it, although one senses that he would still prefer to see these phrases as the simple apposition of nouns.[22] Fitzgerald's main contribution was his explication of the use of similar epithets or titles for goddess and cities in West Semitic sources outside the Bible, which he related to the biblical personification of cities as women, where similar titles are used. The convention, according to Fitzgerald, grew out of the polytheistic idea of the city, or the city goddess, as the consort of the main deity. In Israel this idea was no longer operative—the only traces of it being these titular expressions, of whose origin the biblical authors may not have been aware. Fitzgerald's thesis has been widely accepted for decades, but has now received a trenchant critique from Peggy Day that puts the entire thesis in doubt, and with it, Fitzgerald's grammatical analysis.[23]

Magnar Kartveit makes no reference to Fitzgerald, approaching *bat X* from the context of the study of biblical metaphors rather than from the comparison of Semitic religions or literatures. Dissatisfied with the usual grammatical explanations of the phrase, he concludes that *bat,* the *nomen regens,* is the metaphor and that the *nomen rectum* is the reference to which the metaphor is applied. Zion, or Jerusalem, is being described metaphorically as a *bat.*[24] Kartveit offers a new twist but is in agreement with all of the aforementioned scholars that *bat X* is not to be understood as a true genitive construction and meaning.

F.W. Dobbs-Allsopp has gone against this stream of grammatical explanation and has recently argued for taking *bat X* as a normal construct chain signifying a genitive relationship (genitive of location), "Daughter of City X." He compares Akkadian *marat* + geographic name, an epithet for a goddess linking her to her city, for example, "Daughter of Ur." Dobbs-Allsopp's position that *bat X* is to be associated with divine epithets is not far from Fitzgerald's, but his grammatical analysis differs, giving the phrase a different shade of meaning. Dobbs-Allsopp states that "*bat* in the title *bat* GN, like the Akkadian *martu* in the title *marat* GN, signifies a goddess as an inhabitant or citizen of a particular city or country."[25] Of course, Dobbs-Allsopp understands the biblical use of the title as metaphoric, since no real goddess would be imagined by the biblical author. The texts that he cites for support are "The Hymn of Nana" and a Neo-Babylonian lament for Tammuz. There are several additional references, but it should be noted that this usage is relatively rare and does not occur in the Sumerian city laments or other Sumerian lament literature. Nor do these titles work quite the same way as they do in the West Semitic sources that Fitzgerald cited. A more serious weakness in Dobbs-Allsopp's thesis is that he limits his discussion to cases containing a geographical name.

22. "*Btwlt* and *Bt* as Titles for Capital Cities," 181. See also idem, "The Mythological Background for the Presentation of Jerusalem as Queen."

23. Day, "The Personification of Cities." See also W. Bouzard, *We Have Heard with Our Ears,* 163–69.

24. In an unpublished paper entitled "The Virgin Israel and Her Cognates: Hebrew Construct Chains with Internally Applied Metaphors in the Nomen Regens." I am grateful to Prof. Kartveit for providing me with this paper. See now M. Kartveit, "Sions dotter." *Tidsskrift for Teologi og Kirke* 1–2 (2001): 97–112.

25. "Syntagma of *bat,*" 469–70.

What about *bat-ʿammî,* a phrase similar in usage and construction to *bat* + geographical place? It occurs eight times in Jeremiah, five times in Lamentations, and once in Isaiah, thereby manifesting the same profile of occurrence as the other *bat X* expressions.[26] While Dobbs-Allsopp notes *bat-ʿammî* in passing, the most he can say about it is that "the same basic relationship holds, only the political affiliation has been metonymically shifted from a geographical designation to designation of the people, which results in a slight modification of the title's semantics."[27] I assume that means that Dobbs-Allsopp would analyze *bat-ʿammî* as deriving from the idea of "the goddess who lives among my people," with "people" as a surrogate for the geographic location. But there is no extra-biblical analogy, and at this point the argument becomes forced.

While it would be of interest to know the origin of these expressions, we can understand their use in the Bible without that knowledge (just as we can understand the current meaning of a word without knowing its etymology). Whether and how the word *bat* reflects an early concept of the city goddess (or city as goddess) has not been fully resolved, and I am skeptical about drawing that conclusion. After all, today we refer to countries or cities as female without the implication that this usage derives from the city as a goddess. *Bat-ʿammî* is a personification of the people just as *bat-ṣiyyôn* is a personification of the city. Both phrases have the same grammar, and the best explanation of that grammar remains the appositional genitive. The same holds true for *bĕtûlat yiś-rāʾēl* (Amos 5:2; Jer 31:2, 4) and *bĕtûlat bat X.*

## The Meaning of Bat X

The term *bat* means "daughter," and also "female member of a group" (the feminine counterpart of *bēn*), or "young female, girl." As an epithet of a city, it may be rendered by the somewhat old-fashioned "Lady" or "Fair" ("fair" is archaic English for "woman, lady"), or by "Mademoiselle, Miss." In addition, *bat* connotes an emotional tenderness or protectiveness toward a female person of lesser power or authority. It is a term of endearment, and Stinespring, Kartveit, and others are right to render it as "dear" or its synonyms ("darling, beloved"). It functions like a diminutive: "Dear Little Zion" or "Sweet Little Zion." It can, of course, have an ironic twist when used in certain contexts. *Bat* plus the name of a foreign place (Babylon, Egypt, Edom) is always ironic, and *bat* Zion may at times be ironic (Jer 6:2; Mic 1:13).

Close in meaning and usage is *bĕtûlâ X* and *bĕtûlat bat X. Bĕtûlâ* technically refers to a never-married woman of marriageable age (see commentary on 5:11). It does not connote "chaste, unsullied, virtuous," as "virgin" does in English, but rather a woman in her prime, a woman ripe for marriage.[28] Its metaphoric usage in our expressions may signify pitifulness, much as *bat* does—in both its ironic and nonironic senses. Translations like "poor, dear Zion," "poor little Zion," for *bĕtûlat bat-ṣiyyôn* are possible, although I have retained the more literal "Dear Maiden Zion" in these expressions.

26. Jer 4:11; 6:26; 8:11, 19, 21, 22, 23; 9:6; Lam 2:11; 3:48; 4:3, 6, 10; Isa 22:4. Of similar construction is *bat kaśdîm* in Isa 47:1, 5.

27. "Syntagma of *bat,*" 470 n. 75.

28. Frymer-Kensky translates the phrase as "nubile Zion girl" (*In the Wake of the Goddesses,* 269 n. 7).

## Excursus 2
## Jerusalem's Residents: A Sociological Profile

In order to show how far-reaching the suffering was, the poet refers to its effect on various elements of the population, for example, young and old, priest and prophet, women and children. This trope is common in the Sumerian city laments as well, where, because of the repetitive nature of Sumerian poems, there are lists of those affected by the city's destruction and the way in which they are affected. For example, the Lamentation over the Destruction of Sumer and Ur, lines 12–16, says:

> That the mother does not seek out her child,
> That the father does not say, "Oh, my (dear) wife!"
> That the junior wife does not take joy in (his) embrace,
> That the young child not grow vigorous on (her) knee,
> That the wetnurse not sing lullabies.

Lamentations has a few similar passages, for instance, 2:21: "Lying on the ground in the streets are young and old. My maidens and youths have fallen by the sword." But the Bible tends to use the list form less than Sumerian poetry. Nevertheless, scattered through the five chapters of Lamentations are many references to the population from which one can piece together a cross-section of the inhabitants of Jerusalem. Not every category of resident is included, nor is there necessarily a true sense of the proportion of one category to another. One would expect more emphasis on those whose suffering evokes the greatest sympathy—the young and the women—and they are indeed mentioned quite often. At the other end of the spectrum are society's leaders—priests, prophets, elders—who are also affected by the tragedy, and who at times are blamed for it. The picture that emerges may be of interest from a sociological perspective, so I have collected a list of inhabitants mentioned in the book. (The singular form is generally listed, even when the term occurs only in the plural, except for a few expressions. The list does not include non-Jerusalemites, like the enemy and the passersby.)

>ʾāb (5:3, 7): father, ancestor. In Lamentations they are notable for
> their absence.
>ʾābîr (1:15): warrior, strong man.
>ʾādām (3:36, 39): a person, a human being, without respect to
> gender.
>ʾōhēb (1:2): lover, or in the political sense, ally.
>ʾalmānâ (1:1; 5:3): widow. A woman who has lost her husband and
> thereby her protection in society.
>ʾēm (2:12; 5:3): mother.
>ʾāsîr (3:34): prisoner.
>ʾiššâ, pl. nāšîm (2:20; 4:10; 5:11): woman or married woman. The
> term can be a general designation for adult women or specifi-
> cally for married women.
> bāḥûr (1:15, 18; 2:21; 5:13, 14): young man, youth. A postadoles-
> cent unmarried male.
> bēn (1:16): child.

*běnê ʾîš* (3:33): human beings.

*bětûlâ* (1:4, 18; 2:10, 21; 5:11): a young woman of marriageable age who is not yet married. She is the female counterpart of the *bāḥûr*, the young man (postadolescent). The *bětûlâ* is twice associated with mourning (1:4; 2:10), as she is in Joel 1:8 (where the unmarried woman laments the husband of her youth that she was supposed to have married).

*geber* (3:1, 27, 39): a man. The term stresses the maleness of the person.

*zāqēn* (1:19; 2:20, 21; 4:16; 5:12, 14): elder. One of the respected classes of society. Not necessarily aged.

*ḥālāl* (2:12; 4:9): wounded person (pierced).

*kōhēn* (1:4, 19; 2:1, 20; 4:13, 16): priest. One of the leaders of society, along with the *nābîʾ* and the *zāqēn*.

*kol ʿam* (1:11; 3:14[?]): the general population.

*měʾāhēb* (1:19): lover. See *ʾōhēb*.

*melek* (2:6, 9): king.

*měnaḥēm* (1:2, 9, 16, 17, 21): one who provides comfort to the mourner.

*nābîʾ* (2:9, 14, 20; 4:13): prophet. Often listed with *kōhēn*.

*niddâ* (1:17): menstruating woman, considered ritually impure.

*nāzîr* (4:7): a noble, an aristocrat. To be distinguished from a nazirite—one who has taken a vow of religious devotion that includes not drinking wine, not cutting the hair, and not coming in contact with impurity (see note on 4:7).

*naʿar* (2:21; 5:13): young person, as opposed to an old person. The term often seems to refer to an age bracket but it cannot be precisely determined. The term has a wide range of usages (see H. F. Fuhs, "naʿar," *TDOT* 9:474–85).

*ʿiwwēr* (4:14): blind.

*ʿôlēl* (1:5; 2:11, 19, 20; 4:4): little child, toddler beyond the age of nursing.

*pālîṭ* (2:22): one who escapes.

*ṣaddîq* (4:13): righteous person.

*śar* (1:6; 2:9; 5:12): prince. A leader, mentioned with king and elder.

*śārîd* (2:22): one who remains. A survivor.

*ṭāmēʾ* (4:15): one in a state of ritual impurity.

*yeled* (4:10): child, without reference to age.

*yôneq* (2:11; 4:4): baby, suckling. Mentioned with the *ʿolel*.

*yôṣēr* (4:2): potter.

*yātôm* (5:3): an orphan, one without a father.

The terms fall into several categories. There are terms signaling family status or relationships, like the mother, the widow, the little child, and the maiden. Other terms are from the political realm, like prince, king, elder, and aristocrat; or from the religious realm, such as prophet and priest. It is difficult, and perhaps unwarranted, to distinguish between political and religious leadership, since that distinction is a modern one and did not pertain to the same extent in ancient Israel. Then there are other types of identifications, perhaps best called "the unfortunate," including those with temporary or permanent disabilities: the blind, the menstruant (and others in a state of ritual impurity), the wounded, and the prisoner (the orphan and the widow could be classified here, too). A few general terms occur, like *kol hāʿām*, "the general population," and a few terms especially tailored for the subject matter of the book: lover, escapee, survivor. The ways in which the citizens of Jerusalem are designated is surprisingly diverse, and entirely appropriate for a book that gives multiple perspectives on the destruction. This diversity stands in contrast to the absence of political terminology in Second Isaiah's portrayal of the exilic community. Despite the fact that the exilic community was largely composed of Jerusalem's elite, when Second Isaiah appropriated the language of Lamentations and reversed it, "only the affectively positive language of kinship, not the ambivalent language of leadership, is selected."[29]

### 3. Mourning as a Religious Concept

The first and most central theme of Lamentations is mourning. It emerges in the very first image, the widowed city seeking comfort (1:1–2), followed by the mourning of Zion's roads (1:4), and later the mourning of the elders and the maidens (2:10).[30] While mourning is most evident in chapters 1 and 2, it is pervasive throughout the book and is not limited to the mention of specific ritual or ceremonial behaviors (fasting, abstaining from sexual relations, lamenting, putting ashes or dust on one's head, wearing sackcloth or torn clothing, and sitting on the ground). Mourning is not only a set of customs relating to death, it is an abstract religious concept that had an important place in Israelite cultic thought. The book of Lamentations incorporates the concept of mourning in a number of ways.

The most helpful presentation of both the behavioral and the symbolic aspects of joy and mourning is by Gary Anderson, and I draw on it for the observations that follow.[31] As a religious concept, joy is associated with sacrificial feasting, especially in Deuteronomy (see Deut 12:11–12; 27:7). Conversely, mourning is associated with the absence of sacrificing. Since sacrifice and praise of God are parallel activities, it follows that joy is associated with praising God, as is often expressed in Psalms (e.g., Pss 34:3; 35:21). The mourner, who cannot participate in public joy, is not permitted access to the temple; and his cultic double, the lamenter in psalms of lament, does not praise God during his time of trouble; rather, he hopes to be able to praise God in the future, after he has been delivered from trouble. Psalm 71:20–24 exemplifies this sequence. The psalmist relies on God to help him, to raise him from the depths and to comfort him. The

29. C. Newsom, "Response to Norman K. Gottwald," *Semeia* 59 (1992): 77.

30. Pham (*Mourning in the Ancient Near East and the Hebrew Bible*) finds mourning to be the key to interpreting chaps. 1 and 2, which she explains as being based on the mourning ceremony.

31. *A Time to Mourn*. The topics I mention can be found on the following pages in Anderson: the association with sacrifices (14–19), praising God (38–43), death (87–97), rejoicing of the enemy (73, 93–94), sexual relations (27).

psalmist, on his part, will then acclaim God in music (i.e., in temple worship), sing God's praise, recite his righteous acts.

In his inability to praise God, the mourner is like the dead, and indeed, mourning is closely associated with death and Sheol. Sheol is not only the place where the dead reside, it is the place where the lamenter feels himself to be— the place experienced while in a state of mourning or lamenting. Only when the lamenter is delivered from his trouble does his state of mourning end, at which time he goes to the temple to sacrifice and/or utter praise to God. Psalm 86:12–13 is one example: "I will praise you, LORD my God, with my whole heart, and may I honor your name forever. For your loyalty overwhelms me, in that you have delivered me from the depths of Sheol." (Cf. also Pss 9:14–15; 71:20) Jonah 2:2–10 also fits this pattern. The prophet calls out "from the belly of Sheol" (which here is in the depths of the sea rather than the earth), where he feels driven away from the eyes of God (v. 5). Just as life was ebbing away, Jonah's prayer reached God, "in your holy temple." The poem ends with "On my part, with the sound of praise I will sacrifice to you. I will fulfill what I vowed." Anderson makes the point that references to death and Sheol in psalms of lament are not simply metaphoric expressions for how bad the psalmist feels. They are, rather, religious concepts being reenacted in the psalms. Descent to Sheol, the nadir of the earth (Amos 9:2), is the structural inversion of going up to the temple, the symbolic entryway to heaven. To be in Sheol is to be at the furthest remove from God. Death and mourning, as religious concepts, mean to be cut off from God, just as life and joy mean to be in God's presence.

It should become immediately clear that within this conceptual worldview, the destruction of the temple—a permanent and national denial of access to God—becomes an occasion for public mourning. The destruction is a national death and all Judeans are mourners. The death is a political death, in that the country of Judah ceased to be independent, but it is also a religious death, in the sense of being cut off from access to God's presence. Being in exile only rein- forces the distance from God and the temple, so it is natural that after 586 B.C.E., exile becomes the new Sheol (see commentary on 3:5–9). It is clear from Zech 7:5 and 8:19 that fasting, a ritual of public mourning, was instituted to com- memorate the temple's destruction. Lamentations can be seen as a counterpart to fasting; it is the lamenting part of the mourning ceremony. Moreover, not only is the entire book a lament, it is expressed in such a way that it perpetuates the state of mourning. Deliverance is even more remote than in the psalms of lament, and not even a promise to praise God is offered. The book holds out no comfort, and denies the existence of a comforter, thereby making the cessation of mourn- ing impossible. Lamentations is a plea for comfort in the form of access to God. The plea throughout the book is that God should hear, see, remember, pay atten- tion, and, at its climax, that he should "take us back" (5:21); but the plea is never answered, God remains distant, and so the state of mourning cannot end.

Anderson (*Time to Mourn,* 84) explains that "to comfort" (*nḥm*) has two meanings: to assume the state of mourning along with the mourner, and to bring about the cessation of mourning. Family and friends were obligated to comfort a mourner by joining him as he mourned, to share his loss (as Job's friends did). The kinship model of comfort was applied on the international level, where allies were called "brothers," and where "lovers" (covenant allies) came to aid beleaguered treaty partners. In the case of Judah, her "lovers" deserted her in her time of need, refusing to offer her comfort (1:2, 9, 16). Worse than that, the enemies rejoiced at Jerusalem's sad fate (2:17; 4:21). To rejoice while another is in mourning is to declare oneself an enemy, for this behavior is the antithesis of what a friend is supposed to do. The rejoicing of the enemy should be understood as part of the symbolism of mourning.

Mourning is also associated with abstaining from sexual relations, and the end of the period of mourning with the resumption of sexual relations, as in the case of David and Bathsheba after the death of their child (2 Sam 12:24), and Isaac after the death of Sarah (Gen 24:67). This aspect, too, is implicit in Lamentations in a metaphoric way, because the relationship between God and Israel is conceptualized as that of husband and wife. The personification of Jerusalem as a widow and as an adulterous woman carries with it the implication that this woman is denied sexual relations by her husband—another, albeit less obvious, way of saying that Israel is cut off from God. Isaiah 54:4–6 reverses the image. The shame of adultery and widowhood is removed, the forsaken wife is taken back. This Isaianic passage is just one among many others in which the message of comfort includes the removal of the signs of mourning and the resumption of joy. Isaiah 51:3 sees the reversal of the wilderness of exile and the reinstitution of temple sacrifice ("gladness and joy, thanksgiving and the sound of music"); Jerusalem will rise from sitting in the dust and clothe herself in festive garments (52:1). Choice food will be eaten (55:2) and the exiles will return in joy (55:12). Second Isaiah, who alludes in many places to Lamentations, is responding to the overarching concept of mourning that informs that book.

## 4. The Theology of Destruction and Exile

God, sin, punishment, repentance, faith, hope—all of these are important concepts in Lamentations and all are the stuff from which a theology is made.[32] Yet

---

32. A number of studies have been devoted to the theology of Lamentations, including Gottwald, *Studies in the Book of Lamentations*; Bertil Albrektson, *Studies in the Text and Theology of the Book of Lamentations* (Lund: Gleerup, 1963); Michael S. Moore, "Human Suffering in Lamentations," *RB* 90 (1983): 534–55. These and others are critiqued in Provan, 20–25, and I will not discuss them further.

the book does not construct a theology of its own, nor does it present in any systematic way the standard theology of its time. It assumes the "theology of destruction" in which destruction and exile are the punishment for sin (cf. Deut 4:26–27; 28:32–67; 29:23–27; 30:17–18). The sin that warranted such severe punishment is idolatry, the code word for the rejection of God and his commandments.

Now that punishment has arrived. It marks the most horrendous national catastrophe in the history of Judah, the most colossal break in the entire relationship between God and Israel since its beginning. The very foundations of Judah have crumbled: the country has been conquered, the Davidic monarchy brought to an end, the temple destroyed, and the people exiled from their land. No matter that Deuteronomy had envisioned it and the prophets had foretold it; nothing could prepare one for the cruel reality and the apparent finality of the situation. The burden of Lamentations is not to question why this happened, but to give expression to the fact that it did. At certain moments the book seems to look beyond the destruction, to hold out hope for the future, but in the end despair overcomes hope. Past and future have little place in the book. It centers on the "present"—the moment of trauma, the interminable suffering.[33] The book is not an explanation of suffering but a re-creation of it and a commemoration of it.

Why immortalize this moment of destruction? Because in its own way it signals the truth of the Bible's theology, and it points to the continuation of the covenant between God and Israel. Deuteronomy 30:1–5 envisions the return after the destruction: "When all these things befall you . . . and you take them to heart amidst all the nations to which the LORD your God has banished you" (NJPS). It is that moment of banishment that Lamentations captures, the moment of "taking to heart," and implicit in it is the idea of return (cf. also Deut 4:27–31). Alan Mintz has put it well:

> Destruction, according to the covenant, is a sign neither of God's abandonment of Israel and the cancellation of His obligations to the people, nor of God's eclipse by competing powers in the cosmos. The Destruction is to be taken, rather, as a deserved and necessary punishment for sin. . . . As a chastisement, the Destruction becomes an expression of God's continuing concern for Israel, since the suffering of the Destruction expiates the sins that provoked it and allows a penitent remnant to survive in a rehabilitated and restored relationship with God.[34]

This explains why the poet can cry out to God and expect a response, why he can vent his anger at God, why he can declare that God continues to exist even though his temple does not (Lam 5:18–19), why God is portrayed as so strong and the enemy gets no credit for the destruction. The suffering is, as it were, an affirmation that God is still there and still concerned with the fate of Israel. He

---

33. See Mintz, *Hurban*, 3; Linafelt, *Surviving Lamentations*, 4; Moore, "Human Suffering."
34. Mintz, *Hurban*, 3.

may hide his face, but he has not ceased to be Israel's God. Lamentations contains the seeds of comfort and religious rebuilding that the exilic prophets (especially Second Isaiah) developed more fully in the aftermath of the destruction.

### The Paradigm of Purity

While the book does not offer a systematized theological argument, it draws on two paradigms by which ancient Israel expressed its relationship to its land and to its God. One paradigm, as Tikva Frymer-Kensky has convincingly shown, is that of purity and impurity, or in her words, pollution and purgation. This paradigm is found by and large in the Priestly source. The second, a political paradigm, reflects Deuteronomy.[35]

Frymer-Kensky explains the purity paradigm:

> Wrongful acts could cause the pollution of the nation and of the land of Israel. . . .
> There was therefore an ultimate expectation of catastrophic results for the whole
> people, the "purging" of the land by destruction and exile. Pollution was thought
> to be one of the determinants of Israel's history, and the concept of pollution and
> purgation provided a paradigm by which Israel could understand and survive the
> destruction of the Temple.[36]

The biblical system of purity/impurity consists of two types that should be distinguished even though they seem to overlap at a certain point.[37] One type of impurity is ritual impurity, the causes of which are listed in Lev 11–15 and Num 19 (these include men and women with genital discharges, contact with a corpse, and "leprosy"). This is a natural form of impurity that makes the person temporarily unfit to come in contact with the sanctuary or its holy objects. No sin attaches to it. The passage of a specified period of time and the performance of certain rituals bring the state of impurity to an end. The second type of impurity is moral impurity. It is caused by committing the heinous acts that the Bible considers defiling: sexual sins (Lev 18:24–30), idolatry (Lev 19:31; 20:1–3), and bloodshed (Num 35:33–34). Moral impurity degrades the sinner and defiles the land of Israel. It has no expiating ritual; only punishment brings it to an end.[38] The defiled land spews out its inhabitants, so if Israel defiles its land, the land itself will reject them.

---

35. Deuteronomy also speaks of defiling the land (19:10; 20:18; 21:23; cf. 24:4) but not as leading to exile.

36. "Pollution, Purification, and Purgation in Biblical Israel," 399.

37. My discussion is informed by the excellent study of J. Klawans, *Impurity and Sin in Ancient Judaism* (Oxford: Oxford University Press, 2000), 1–42.

38. Moral impurity may be permanent in some cases. In limited cases, the ritual of the Day of Atonement may erase it (Lev 16:11–22). See Klawans, *Impurity,* 26–27 and 30–31.

The concept of the defilement of the land from moral impurity lies behind much of the imagery of Lamentations. Several passages from elsewhere in the Bible help to clarify this idea.

> Do not defile *(ṭāmēʾ)* yourselves in any of those ways, for it is by such that nations that I am casting out before you defiled themselves. Thus the land became defiled; and I called it to account for its iniquity, and the land spewed out its inhabitants. But you must keep my laws . . . and must not do any of those abhorrent things *(tôʿēbâ)* . . . so let not the land spew you out for defiling it. (Lev 18:24–28)

> You shall not pollute the land in which you live; for blood pollutes the land, and the land can have no expiation for blood that is shed on it. You shall not defile the land in which you live, in which I myself abide. (Num 35:33–34)

> They worshiped their idols . . . they shed innocent blood . . . so the land was polluted with bloodguilt. Thus they became defiled by their acts. . . . The Lord was angry with his people and he abhorred his inheritance. He handed them over to the nations; their foes ruled them. (Ps 106:34–41)

> O mortal, arraign, arraign the city of bloodshed; declare to her all her abhorrent deeds. . . . You stand guilty of the blood you have shed, defiled by the fetishes you have made. (Ezek 22:1–4; cf. also Ezek 36:18; Jer 2:23; 3:1)

Lamentations partakes of the same imagery and the same paradigm of moral defilement of the land, and many of the seemingly disconnected images of the book cohere around it, especially and obviously the ones of the sexually immoral woman. These images are not used only, or even primarily, because they are violent and shocking (although they are certainly effective in that regard), but because they have a central role in the paradigm of moral impurity (since one of the leading causes of moral impurity is sexual immorality). That role is both literal, in that the view was that immoral behavior pollutes the land in a literal sense, and figurative, in that the prophets made the morally impure woman (i.e., the sexually wanton woman) into a metaphor for Israel.[39] The paradigm of moral impurity is invoked continually in Lamentations, and the failure to recognize it leads to the misconstrual of the use of sexual imagery in the book.

A different type of metaphorization may also occur on occasion, wherein the terms for ritual impurity are applied to moral impurity. We find this most clearly in Lam 4:15, where the ritually impure leper (Lev 13:45) is the symbol of the morally impure leaders. The poet makes this comparison for the purpose of conveying the untouchability—the utter rejection—of those who have sinned. Some interpreters also see this type of metaphorization in Lam 1:9 and 17, where Zion is compared to a menstruant *(niddâ)*. I argue in the commentary that 1:9 is probably not a reference to menstruation and that in any case exegetes have misun-

---

39. See the discussion of Klawans, *Impurity,* 32–36.

derstood the nature of menstrual impurity. Menstruation, like other genital discharges, causes ritual impurity, but there is no immorality or disgust associated with it (Lev 15:19–24). Nevertheless, it is clear that elsewhere in the Bible ritual impurity can *symbolize* moral impurity. In Ezek 36:17 the menstruant serves as a symbol of moral impurity: "their ways were in my sight like the impurity of the *niddâ.*" Ezra 9:11 refers to the defilement of the land as *niddâ*. Perhaps this metaphor is employed because Israel is personified as a woman, and the shedding of blood is a common element of menstruating women and of moral impurity. However, it should be stressed that this is not the plain-sense meaning of *niddâ* but a metaphorized use. There is nothing immoral about a menstruating woman.[40] Only in a culture where the concept of impurity was thoroughly understood and accepted could the prophets and poets use it in this way. The modern reader needs to appreciate the pervasiveness of the purity/impurity system in biblical thought in order to appreciate its use in Lamentations.

### The Political Paradigm

The second paradigm by which Israel explained the destruction does not come from the sphere of religion but from the sphere of law and international politics. This political paradigm is based on the relationship between suzerain and vassal, best known through the ancient Near Eastern treaties and reflected also in the Assyrian and Babylonian annals. It is the model for the covenant between God and Israel. Deuteronomy is the book that most obviously frames the covenant in terms of a treaty (but cf. also Exod 20–23 and Lev 26). Ancient Near Eastern treaties had sections containing curses—the consequences for disobeying the stipulations of the treaty—and Deuteronomy 28 has been recognized to be patterned on these curses. The language of Deut 28:49–68 bears much resemblance to the descriptions of the war and siege in Lamentations: "The LORD will bring a nation against you from afar. . . . It shall shut you up in all your towns . . . you shall eat your own issue, the flesh of your sons and daughters . . . you shall be torn from the land. . . . The LORD will scatter you among all the peoples" (NJPS). The treaty model helps us to understand why it is God, not the Babylonians, who are blamed for the destruction. It was with God that Israel made the covenant, and it is God, therefore, who is the offended suzerain. The Babylonians do not come into the picture at all.

Just how well the biblical view fits the general ancient Near Eastern picture can be seen from the following excerpt from the Annals of Ashurbanipal.

Famine broke out among them and they ate the flesh of their children against their hunger. Asher, Sin, Shamash, Adad, Bel, Nebo, the Ishtar of Nineveh . . . the Ishtar

40. For other metaphorizations of ritual impurity see Isa 30:22; 64:4–5.

of Arbela, Ninurta, Nergal (and) Nusku (thus) inflicted quickly upon them (all) the curses written (down) in their sworn agreements. . . . Whenever the inhabitants of Arabia asked each other: "On account of what have these calamities befallen Arabia?" (they answered themselves:) "Because we did not keep the solemn oaths (sworn by) Ashur, because we offended the friendliness of Ashurbanipal." (*ANET,* 300)

The primary offense against the suzerain in the real world of the ancient Near East was rebellion, the attempt of the vassal country to break free of the suzerain's control. This would provoke a military campaign to reassert control and would generally include deportation as a punishment. Deportation is best known as an Assyrian practice, mentioned often in the annals, but as early as the Code of Hammurabi we find in the warning against anyone who disobeys the laws: "May he [Enlil] order . . . the destruction of his city, the dispersion of his people, the transfer of his kingdom, the disappearance of his name and memory from the land" (*ANET,* 179, lines 71–73). In the cultural milieu of the ancient Near East, deportation was the normal punishment for rebellion or the breaking of a vassal treaty, and it was natural, then, that rebellion against God would lead to the exile of the people. "My God rejects them, because they have not obeyed him; and they will go wandering among the nations" (Hos 9:17). When the exile of the Judeans actually occurred, the paradigm was in place to explain it as a punishment for rebellion against God.[41]

Both the paradigm of purity and the political paradigm converge in their view that exile is the ultimate punishment for the most serious sins. It is, therefore, easy to understand how prophets and poets could fuse the two paradigms together, as they are in Lamentations.

## 5.   Lamentations in Literary Context

### *The Biblical Context:* **Qinah,** *Communal Lament,* **and *Jerusalem Lament**

When David learns of the death of Absalom, he cries out, "My son, Absalom, my son, my son, O that I had died instead of you, Absalom, my son, my son" (2 Sam 19:1). This is the literary expression of a father's raw grief for his son. David's words are contrived by the author to convey a natural, instinctive outpouring of grief, shock, and despair, bringing to a close the complicated relationship between this father and son. These words are uttered in private; they are personal reactions and are expressed in prose. Such personal outpourings of grief are rare in biblical narrative. More typically, grief or mourning is

---

41. See B. Oded, *Mass Deportations,* 40–41; see also George E. Mendenhall and Gary A. Herion, "Covenant," *ABD* 1:1179–1202; Michael L. Barré, "Treaties in the ANE," *ABD* 6:653–56.

expressed through gestures, without words, as when Jacob mourns the loss of Joseph: "Jacob tore his clothes, put sackcloth on his waist, and mourned for his son many days" (Gen 37:34–35).[42] Public responses to death, on the other hand, while also marked by gestures of mourning, are more likely to be accompanied by speech (like David's lament over Saul and Jonathan in 2 Sam 1 and his shorter lament over Abner in 2 Sam 3:33–34). Since these are formal occasions, the speech is in poetry, for poetry is the Bible's preferred form for public recitation, including public laments.[43]

The term for the biblical funeral dirge or eulogy is *qinah* (pl.: *qinot*). David recited a *qinah* for Saul and Jonathan (2 Sam 1:17) and for Abner (2 Sam 3:33). According to 2 Chr 35:25, Jeremiah lamented or eulogized (*qnn*) the death of Josiah, and other singers had a repertoire of *qinot*; in fact, there was a written collection of them. The Mishnah (*Moed Q.* 3:9) further defines the form of the *qinah* used at funerals in its own time: in a *qinah,* one of the keening women recites and the others repeat after her. Although no actual *qinah* from the biblical period survives (the *qinot* we have in narrative and prophetic discourse are literary creations that presumably imitate actual dirges), we may conclude from numerous references to it that the *qinah* was a well-established genre of poetry used for the public mourning of individuals. When the prophets recite a *qinah* for Israel or another nation, they are lifting the term from its real-life setting and using it as an ironic metaphor for the inevitable death of a nation (e.g., Amos 5:1; Jer 9:9; Ezek 19:1).[44]

The term *qinah* does not appear in the book of Lamentations (in the MT) or in the psalms that lament the destruction of Jerusalem. The use of *qinah* to designate a lamentation other than a funeral dirge is postbiblical, although its antecedents may be seen in the prophets' metaphoric use of the term (e.g., Amos 5:1). Rabbinic literature calls the book of Lamentations *qinot* (*b. B. Bat.* 14b), *měgillat qînôt* (*y. Shab.* 16.15.c) or *sēper qînôt* (*b. Ḥag.* 8b), paralleling the LXX and Vulgate, which title the book by the Greek and Latin equivalent, respectively. This usage reflects the tradition that Lamentations is the same composition by Jeremiah referred to in 2 Chr 35:25. Other biblical texts that are called *qinot* by the rabbis are Psalm 3 (*b. Ber.* 7b) and Psalm 79 (*Lam. Rab.* to IV, ii). Several

42. Gestures or behaviors are the primary way that mourning and joy are indicated in the Bible. See Anderson, *Time to Mourn.* Signs of mourning include fasting, abstaining from sexual relations, wearing sackcloth, putting ashes on the head, and sitting on the ground. Jacob's words in Gen 37:35 do not constitute a lament; they are an expression of his refusal to be comforted.

43. Other types of public recitation for which poetry was used include formal prayer or praise (psalms), wisdom teachings, prophetic speeches, and victory chants. Prose is used for private, or informal, prayers. See M. Greenberg, *Biblical Prose Prayer as a Window to the Popular Religion of Ancient Israel* (Berkeley: University of California Press, 1983).

44. I emphasize that the prophets are invoking the *qinah* genre, not the city-lament genre, as Dobbs-Allsopp claims, most recently in "Darwinism, Genre Theory, and City Laments," 626 n. 17.

centuries later, the term *qinot* came to designate a category of *pîyûṭîm* (liturgical poems) about the destruction of Jerusalem recited on the Ninth of Ab, the day that Jews commemorate the destruction of the First and Second Temples.

The term modern form critics have most consistently applied to Lamentations and to similar biblical poems in the book of Psalms is *communal lament*. This designation is a modern invention, not a biblical term, and was first applied to Psalms, most consistently to Pss 44, 60, 74, 79, 80, 83, 85, 90, 94, 123, and 137.[45] Note that the term *qinah* does not occur in these psalms, and they are not funeral dirges. They are, rather, compositions "used by and/or on behalf of a community to express both complaint, and sorrow and grief over some perceived calamity, physical or cultural, which had befallen or was about to befall them and to appeal to God for deliverance."[46] There are a number of characteristic elements of a communal lament, but the sine qua non is the appeal for deliverance. This makes the communal lament quite different from a biblical *qinah*. A *qinah* is an outpouring of grief for a loss that has already occurred, with no expectation of reversing that loss; a communal lament is a plea to prevent a calamity or to reverse it. The prophets' metaphoric use of *qinah* is entirely apt because they saw the demise of the nation as a fait accompli. They personify the nation as a corpse, over whom a dirge is recited. As Amos says in his *qinah* for the house of Israel, "it is fallen and will not arise . . . no one will raise it up" (Amos 5:1). So it is with Ezekiel's dirges for Tyre (27:2) and for Pharaoh (32:2). Jeremiah (7:29; 9:9, 19) and Ezekiel (19:1, 14; 26:17; 27:2, 32; 28:12; 32:2, 16) are metaphorically mourning a destruction, not appealing for deliverance.

The book of Lamentations has presented problems for form critics who like neat genre categorizations for literary works, for it has elements of the *qinah* and also elements of the communal lament. Like a *qinah*, it mourns for an irreparable loss that has already occurred. At the same time, Lamentations pleads for the restoration of its people, as a communal lament does. Scholars have recognized this combination of genres (plus several others) and have argued about which of the two genres is primary: Is Lamentations a *qinah* with elements of communal lament, or is it a communal lament with *qinah* elements? No easy answer is forthcoming, nor must we choose one genre over the other. Literary works are often of mixed genre, and new ones are continually evolving.

While Lamentations may be related to the *qinah* and to the communal

---

45. So James Limburg, "Psalms, Book of," *ABD* 5:532, with the addition, in parenthesis, of 12, 108, and 129. Bouzard, *We Have Heard*, 102, presents a chart of the lists of thirteen scholars. While there is considerable variety, most agree on 44, 60, 74, 79, 80, and 83. P. Ferris, *The Genre of Communal Lament*, 93, lists 31, 35, 42/43, 44, 56, 59, 60, 74, 77, 79, 80, 83, 85, 89, 94, 102, 109, 137, and the five chapters of Lamentations.

46. Ferris, *Genre*, 10. See also Bouzard, *We Have Heard*, 1–2.

lament, it transcends both those genres and constitutes a new, post-586 type of lament, which I call the Jerusalem lament. Other examples of Jerusalem laments are Pss 74, 79, and 137, and we may also include Pss 44, 69, and 102. This new genre or subgenre arose from a new historical situation and a new theological need. To be sure, city laments existed elsewhere in the ancient Near East long before 586 (see the discussion below on Mesopotamian laments). And certainly Jerusalem was not the first city in Israel or Judah to suffer destruction. But contra some recent proposals, there is no compelling evidence for the use of city laments for destroyed Israelite or Judean cities before the destruction of Jerusalem.[47] Even if there had been such laments, there would be a qualitative difference between them and the Jerusalem lament, because Jerusalem occupied a special place in biblical religious thought. The historical and theological implications of Jerusalem's destruction go beyond those of any earlier destruction, at least in the Judean view, for what is at stake is the existence of Judean national and religious identity.

The Jerusalem lament is more than simply a combination of the *qinah* and the communal lament, although both these types of poems may have paved the way for it. Another genre of poems that should be brought into the discussion is "Zion songs," a modern form-critical label drawn from Ps 137:3 that also includes Pss 46, 48, 50, 76, 84, 87, and 122.[48] These poems are odes to Zion, delighting in its beauty, its religious significance, and its physical structures. But when Zion's physical structures are destroyed and the future of its religious role is in doubt, singing a Zion song becomes problematic. As Ps 137 says, one cannot sing a Zion song in exile. Psalm 137 is a silencing of Zion songs, a poetic refusal to sing, and a poem about the impossibility of singing a Zion song when Jerusalem is destroyed.

Gary Anderson's investigation into the religious phenomenology of joy and mourning provides further insight into the meaning of Ps 137 and the cessation

---

47. I am not persuaded by the argument of Dobbs-Allsopp, *Weep, O Daughter of Zion*, reiterated in "Darwinism," that city laments were used in Israel before 586 B.C.E. See my review in *JAOS* 115 (1995): 319. This idea was mentioned by Hillers, 35 (Dobbs-Allsopp was Hillers's student). More recently E. Greenstein ("The Lament"), who accepts and builds on Dobbs-Allsopp's thesis, has suggested that remnants of such a lament may be found in Ps 78:59–66. This psalm does, indeed, contain some elements similar to Lamentations, although it is clearly not a lament in its current form. (I discuss Ps 78 in a forthcoming article, "Lamenting Jerusalem in the Psalms" in *The Book of Psalms: Composition and Reception* to be published by Brill.) The question is whether lament-sounding language in prophetic speech or psalms proves that these elements originated in a city-lament genre. All it proves, in my opinion, is that certain motifs connected with war and destruction were widely used and are not genre-specific (see my discussion below).

48. Albrektson, *Studies,* 224–30, also discusses Zion songs in relation to Lamentations, but primarily for theological reasons. He sees the idea of the inviolability of Jerusalem as stemming from these songs. To be sure, he also sees literary connections, even allusions, that Lamentations makes to Zion songs, but his focus is on theological links rather than literary development.

of Zion songs after the destruction. Zion songs are one of many public rituals of joy, along with appearing in God's presence and praising him. A mourner or penitent was not permitted to engage in public joy, and a person cut off from God was considered a mourner. After the destruction of Jerusalem, all Judeans were, in this sense, mourners, for they had lost access to God. They were therefore forbidden to sing praises to God or Zion, as their captors tauntingly requested (Ps 137:2).[49] What, then, could they sing? What could take the place of Zion songs? Psalm 137 transforms the Zion song into the Jerusalem lament, or, more properly, in Ps 137 we see the demise of Zion songs and the birth of Jerusalem laments. The Jerusalem laments are the antithesis of Zion songs; they are songs for the lost Zion.[50] Lamentations is the Jerusalem lament par excellence.

Clearly, poems lamenting Jerusalem must be dated after 586, and hence the few Psalms that do so are dated to the postdestruction period. By contrast, the communal laments that express only a vague complaint of unspecified danger and make no reference to the exile are dated by most scholars to the preexilic period. If this dating is accurate, a major difference exists between pre- and postexilic communal laments. All postexilic communal laments are laments for the destruction of Jerusalem and/or the exile of the people. To put it another way, communal laments in the exilic and postexilic periods have as their "complaint," or as background to their current complaint, the destruction of Jerusalem. It is but a small step from Jerusalem lament to postexilic penitential prayer, where the theme of exile continues, enduring even after the return to Judah and the rebuilding of the temple.[51]

### *The Mesopotamian Context*

The relationship between the Sumerian city laments and the book of Lamentations has been discussed in most studies of Lamentations since the Sumerian compositions came to light. More recently, the discussion has been broadened to include other compositions, especially the *eršemma* and *balag*

49. Anderson, *Time to Mourn,* 43.

50. I note, without implying any direct connection, that the Sumerians had temple hymns, poems glorifying their temples, which might be considered roughly parallel to Zion songs. The Sumerians also wrote laments for their destroyed cities (and their temples) that are often compared to Lamentations. Neither temple hymns nor city laments are much in evidence among Akkadian poems. It may be, then, that the composing of city laments is in some way related to the existence of temple hymns.

51. See M. Knibb, "The Exile in the Literature of the Intertestamental Period," *HeyJ* 17 (1976): 253–72; and R. A. Werline, *Penitential Prayer in Second Temple Judaism,* SBLEJL 13 (Atlanta: Scholars Press, 1998). For the theme of exile in early rabbinic literature, see C. Milikowsky, "Notions of Exile, Subjugation and Return in Rabbinic Literature," in *Exile: Old Testament, Jewish, and Christian Conceptions,* ed. J. Scott, JSJSup 56 (Leiden: Brill, 1997), 265–96.

prayers.[52] The discussion has largely revolved around the question of whether there was direct influence or borrowing, or whether the similarities between the two lament traditions are to be explained as part of a more diffuse ancient Near Eastern literary tradition in response to destruction. Thomas F. McDaniel argued that the similarities between the Sumerian city laments and the biblical Lamentations did not prove direct influence but were two independent manifestations of a broad literary tradition of laments. W. C. Gwaltney Jr. took the opposite position, arguing that the gap in time and geographical distance between Sumer and Israel could be bridged if one took into account the first-millennium Sumerian *eršemma* and *balag* compositions, which he saw as a link in the chain of direct influence between Sumerian laments and the book of Lamentations.[53] Most recently, F. W. Dobbs-Allsopp has suggested that, while the origins of city laments are in Sumer, the genre was known in Israel some two centuries before the destruction of Jerusalem.[54] Dobbs-Allsopp thereby minimizes the Mesopotamian influence by placing it at a greater remove from Lamentations, which, according to him, emerged from a lament tradition that had already become an Israelite one. The question of literary borrowing from Mesopotamia remains unresolved, with opinion divided on the nature and extent of Sumerian influence. A parallel discussion exists regarding communal laments in Psalms and the Sumerian *balag* and *eršemma* compositions (and several other types of Sumerian prayers). Here, too, views differ, with Paul Ferris taking the position that one may place the Sumerian and Hebrew prayers on a historical-cultural continuum but that the evidence does not support a direct borrowing. Walter C. Bouzard Jr., on the other hand, is more inclined to see a specific literary connection, although the evidence remains circumstantial.[55]

Whatever their historical relationship may be, Mesopotamian lament literature and the book of Lamentations obviously share similar motifs, themes, and images. These range from general descriptions of destruction to specific images

52. For the texts of the Sumerian city laments see Green, "The Eridu Lament"; idem, "The Uruk Lament"; S. N. Kramer, "Lamentation over the Destruction of Ur," *ANET*, 455–63; Michalowski, *The Lamentation over the Destruction of Sumer and Ur*; Tinney, *The Nippur Lament*. A sixth lament, for the destruction of Ekimar, has not, to my knowledge, been published. Also to be included in the discussion is "The Curse of Agade" (J. Cooper, *The Curse of Agade*), although it is generally thought of as historiography or political propaganda rather than a lament. An overview of Mesopotamian lament literature is presented by Hallo, "Lamentations and Prayers in Sumer and Akkad." For a recent survey of research on the relationship of the city laments to Lamentations see Dobbs-Allsopp, *Weep*, 2–10.

53. W. C. Gwaltney Jr., "The Biblical Book of Lamentations in the Context of Near Eastern Lament Literature"; T. F. McDaniel, "The Alleged Sumerian Influence upon Lamentations."

54. His original position was articulated in *Weep*, which I reviewed in *JAOS* 115 (1995): 319. Dobbs-Allsopp has clarified some of his terminology in "Darwinism."

55. Ferris, *Genre*, 174; Bouzard, *We Have Heard*, 201, 210.

and phrases—lists of members of society who suffered, the physical and architectural structures destroyed, the ravages of famine and even cannibalism, the loss of temple and its rites, and the explanation of the catastrophe by the decision of the gods to abandon the city and to permit the enemy to conquer it. Pointing out these similarities allows us to see Lamentations in a larger literary context, and in some cases to grasp the imagery more clearly. (For example, see the commentary on 1:20.) These similarities show, at the very least, that widely used conventional themes and language for speaking of war and destruction persisted throughout the ancient Near East. Moreover, these conventions are not limited to laments, but are also found in other genres, for example, in Assyrian annals and in treaty curses and in the curses of Deut 28 and in prophetic warnings. *These shared themes and motifs are not specific to the genre of laments.* The point should be emphasized, because all too often the lament genre is defined, at least in part, by the presence of these motifs. This, in turn, muddies the waters in discssions of the origin and development of the lament genre.

Rather than inquire further into the origin of Lamentations, or the degree of Mesopotamian influence on it, I prefer to take as a given the cultural context of which Lamentations is a part and in which it should be read. The nations of the ancient Near East shared a general view of what happens when a people disobeyed its overlord/Lord. They constructed the punishment resulting from this breach in similar terms, picturing the antithesis of what they valued as a society: family and its continuity through progeny and inheritance; peaceful life in one's own land; economic prosperity; physical well-being; and the ongoing observance of the proper religious rites. To paraphrase Robert Browning, God's in his temple, all's right with the world. This ideal is turned on its head as a threat in treaty curses and as a fait accompli in lament literature.

Thus the specifically Judean context includes songs praising Jerusalem, a multifaceted ancient Near Eastern literature of lament, a Judean notion of sin and punishment, and conventional ways for conceptualizing war, defeat, and destruction. Future studies should ask: How did the poet of Lamentations use the common or stereotypical motifs at his disposal? In what ways do the distinctive history and religion of Israel affect the use of shared ancient Near Eastern forms of expression? These are questions about cultural contexts and comparisons, rather than questions about the lineage of laments.

Although I have stressed the conventional nature of many of the forms of expression that Lamentations shares with the Sumerian city laments (and other literature), I should also note certain major differences between the Sumerian and Judean situations. The Sumerians lived under a political arrangement in which one city at a time had hegemony over a large territory, and when that city declined, hegemony passed to another city. The Sumerians speak of this in terms of the transfer of kingship to another place (a principle expressed in the Sumerian King List by the phrase "its kingship was carried away" or "its kingship was carried to city X"). For them, the rise and fall of cities was the norm and needed no special explanation. As the Lamentation over the Destruction of Sumer and Ur, lines 366–70, puts it,

> Ur was indeed given kingship (but) it was not given an eternal reign.
> From time immemorial, since the land was founded, until the population multiplied,
> Who has ever seen a reign of kingship that would take precedence (for ever)?
> The reign of its kingship had been long indeed but had to exhaust itself.
> O my Nanna, do not exert yourself (in vain), leave your city![56]

Thus is the fall of the Ur III dynasty justified. The gods have decreed that its end had come not as a punishment, but because it was in the nature of things that no dynasty lasts forever. The Sumerian composition is an apologia, a justification of the founder of the Isin dynasty who destroyed the city of Ur and then rebuilt it even as he superseded the Ur III dynasty. Nothing could be further from the Judean theology of the destruction of Jerusalem and the Davidic dynasty. The Davidic dynasty was eternal; David's descendants were destined to sit on the throne of Judah forever (2 Sam 7:12–16). No precedent exists, in theory or in history, for the Davidic dynasty to be superseded.[57] Even when the kingdom is divided, God reserves one kingdom for David's descendants. When Nebuchadnezzar took upon himself to appoint a king of Judah, he appointed Zedekiah, a member of the Davidic family. Second Kings ends on a note of hope for the future continuity of Judah with the notice that its legitimate king, Jehoiachin, was alive and well in Babylonia. Later, the idea of Davidic kingship is transmuted into messianic thought. Kingship in Judah (actual or metaphorical) becomes unthinkable without a Davidic ruler. It is likewise unthinkable without Jerusalem as its capital, the capital founded by David and permanently linked with his dynasty. Jeremiah had to work very hard to convince his audience that Jerusalem was not inviolable (Jer 7). To find a precedent for the possible destruction of Jerusalem he had to look all the way back to Shiloh. The destruction of the northern kingdom could not serve as a precedent because, in Judean theology, that kingdom and its capitals and sanctuaries were never fully legitimate to begin with (see 2 Kgs 17). The notion that God would abandon his city was inconceivable, whereas in the Sumerian lamentation the god of Ur, Nanna, is told to leave. The destruction of Jerusalem and the end of the Davidic dynasty were much harder for Judeans to accept and justify than the destruction of a Sumerian city and the end of its dynasty were for Sumerians.

---

56. Michalowski, *Lamentation,* 59. See his discussion on pp. 14–15 of this justification of the destruction of Ur.

57. To be sure, Saul's dynasty was superseded (2 Sam 7:15), but that is not pictured as happening again in Judah. As for the northern kingdom of Israel, no lasting dynasty was ever established.

Another important difference is that the policy of deporting conquered populations was begun by the Assyrians, long after the time of the Sumerian laments. Although the notion of the dispersion of conquered people predates the Assyrian policy, and there were certainly captives of war (see the epilogue of the Code of Hammurabi, lines 70–80; Lamentation over the Destruction of Ur, lines 283–85; Nippur Lament, line 215), the Sumerians did not have to deal with the trauma of the wholesale exile of a people or its theological implications. Only the gods leave the Sumerian cities, not the people. The gods return when the city temple is rebuilt and rededicated, which was, as best as scholars can discern, the occasion for the recitation of the city laments. So the Sumerian laments have a happy ending. They celebrate the reversal of the destructions that they describe. Lamentations has no such happy ending. The destruction is not reversed, but rather rehearsed over and over again. God has abandoned his people, and the sense of this abandonment permeates the composition.[58]

## 6. Authorship

Various ancient traditions assign the authorship of biblical and extrabiblical writings to specific personages. In the Bible itself we find ascriptions of psalms and poems to named individuals, and certain books as a whole are by virtue of their superscriptions linked with their putative authors—the prophetic books, Song of Songs, and the like. This trend grows even stronger in postbiblical sources. The rabbis assigned authors to all biblical books, whether or not such authorship was explicitly stated in the biblical text. For example, Samuel wrote Judges, Ruth, and Samuel; and Jeremiah was the author of Kings, Jeremiah, and Lamentations (*b. B Bat.* 14b–15a).[59] While the MT does not make the Jeremian authorship of Lamentations explicit by means of a superscription, the LXX and Vulgate do. In these versions, the book opens with the words: "And it came to pass after Israel had gone into captivity, and Jerusalem was laid waste, that Jeremiah sat weeping and composed this lament over Jerusalem and said. . . ."

The tradition of linking Lamentations with Jeremiah is quite ancient and pervasive. The earliest hint of this tradition is in 2 Chr 35:25: "Jeremiah recited laments for Josiah and all the male and female singers said (them) in their laments for Josiah, until today. They became accepted custom in Israel and they were recorded in the laments." According to a long exegetical tradition, the "laments" (*haqqînôt*) mentioned in this verse are none other than the book of

---

58. See Dobbs-Allsopp, "Tragedy, Tradition, and Theology," 33.

59. Jewish tradition (see Rashi) tries to pin down the writing of the book even further, suggesting that three chapters of Lamentations were written by Jeremiah on the scroll that Jehoiakim burned, and that later Jeremiah rewrote it and added more (Jer 36:32). However, Ibn Ezra rejects this notion, noting that Lamentations does not contain a mention of Babylonia or of Nebuchadnezzar (which was in Jeremiah's scroll), and therefore could not be the document referred to in Jer 36.

Lamentations (called *qinot* in rabbinic literature). One cannot be sure that the Chronicler was referring specifically to the book of Lamentations itself, but clearly a biblical tradition connecting Jeremiah with lament literature exists.

Ancient traditions and modern scholars have different reasons for assigning authorship to biblical books. The rabbis, and presumably their forerunners, were interested in showing the divine or sacred nature of the biblical writings, and in order to do this they link the books with prophetic figures or with other people who composed under divine inspiration (like David, Solomon, and Ezra). They make "logical" and "chronological" connections: the books written by Samuel are those set in the period in which Samuel lived; the books with superscriptions linking them to Solomon reflect Solomon's attribute of wisdom; and so forth. In the process of ascribing books to authors, they make Scripture a more coherent unity, for even the small anonymous books in the Writings become integrated with earlier personalities and writings. The Christian canons achieve a similar end by actually placing books together by putative author: Ruth is placed before Samuel; and Proverbs, Ecclesiastes, and Song of Songs (the Solomonic writings) are grouped together. Jewish and Christian traditions of authorship are similar, but they manifest themselves differently. The Christian canonical order that places Lamentations after Jeremiah reflects the same ancient tradition of Jeremian authorship for Lamentations that is found in rabbinic writings. The MT ordering of books, however, puts Lamentations in the Writings, among the Five Scrolls, grouped together because they are used liturgically on special days during the year. Lamentations is recited on 9 Ab, the commemoration of the destruction of both the First and Second Temples.

Modern scholars approach the question of authorship quite differently. Nothing would delight scholars more than knowing who actually wrote a certain book, but because that goal is largely out of reach, they must content themselves with trying to establish which group of people, or which school, is most likely to have produced certain types of literature. This, in turn, depends on the dating of the texts. In the case of Lamentations, a date during or slightly after the time of Jeremiah is accepted by many scholars, making Jeremian authorship in theory possible. Moreover, Jeremiah and Lamentations share similar language. This is not to say, however, that modern scholars conclude that Jeremiah himself wrote Lamentations, although many speak in terms of a Jeremian school, or more broadly, a Deuteronomistic school (of which Jeremiah is a part). On the other hand, there have been objections to Jeremian authorship based on the inconsistencies between Jeremiah's view of the destruction and that expressed by the poet of Lamentations. Jeremiah had clearly predicted the destruction, yet the poet seems shocked by it; Jeremiah warned of the sins of the people, yet this gets little emphasis in Lamentations. The poet of Lamentations accuses God of intense anger, of too harsh punishment, of abandoning his people—things that seem very different from Jeremiah's prophecies. One might respond to these arguments by observing that Jeremiah's prophecies came before the destruction while Lamentations comes after it, so a different tone and outlook would be expected even if the same person wrote both books. A skillful author need not always sound the same or use the same style and language.[60]

The point I wish to make is not which side of this argument has greater merit, but that to frame the question this way is meaningless. Given that there is no evidence on which to discover the actual author, what we are really doing, from a literary perspective, is reconstructing the implied author of the text, the image of authorship projected by the text. The implied author is a fictive persona, not a historical individual—a persona who is not quite the same as, but yet not wholly separable from, the speaking voices in the text.[61] Just as in biblical narrative it is largely impossible to distinguish the implied author from the narrator, so in biblical poetry it is impossible to distinguish the implied author from the poet, the voice or voices that speak the poems.

These speaking voices have received considerable attention in recent studies.[62] Some scholars find a new voice or set of voices in each chapter, while others find the same voice in several chapters. One of the voices is that of Jerusalem, and surely no one thinks that the city is an author in any real sense. Yet discussions of the first-person singular voice in chapter 3 all too often merge the question of authorship with implied poet. The speaker of chapter 3 is no more real than Jerusalem, a speaker in chapter 1. To bring us full circle, a recent study by Nancy C. Lee suggests that there are two primary poets in Lamentations. One is a female lamenter, sometimes called "Dear Zion," and the other is a prophet who uses formulaic prophetic rhetoric. Lee identifies that prophet with Jeremiah, since she finds a great deal of common language in Lamentations and the book of Jeremiah. For her, Jeremiah is not the "author" in the literal sense but "a poet among others featured in Lamentations."[63] That is to say, Jeremiah is a poetic persona whose voice may be heard in Lamentations, perhaps even the preeminent persona of the book (the implied author or narrator). To put it another way: If we hear a speaking voice in the book, and that voice uses the language and imagery of Jeremiah, who better to imagine uttering those words than Jeremiah, the same persona of the book of Jeremiah, the prophet of the destruction and exile par excellence? We may find an analogy in the book of Jonah, where the prophet Jonah is the implied author but certainly not the real, historical author. Perhaps the author of Lamentations has used the persona of Jeremiah in a manner analogous to the way the author of the book of Jonah has used the persona of the prophet named Jonah. The dominant "poet" of our book is not the author in a historical sense, but is, rather, the implied author in the literary sense.

60. See the discussion in Provan, 9–19.
61. See Provan, 18–19.
62. See Lanahan, "Speaking Voice."
63. Lee, *The Singers of Lamentations*, 3.

## 7. Date and Purpose

Most scholars date Lamentations to a time soon after 586 B.C.E.[64] It cannot be earlier; the question is how much later might it be. The view that it was written soon after the destruction used to be justified by the fact that the descriptions are so vivid that they must have been composed by eyewitnesses. This reasoning betrays a simplistic notion of literature. A good poet can convey immediacy even if he was not present. The depth of feeling that the poem calls forth has nothing to do with its date. In fact, there are both ancient and modern examples of destruction literature composed some time after the events, as well as examples composed during or immediately following them. I offer the following three examples.

1. The Sumerian city laments, which sound as much like eyewitness accounts as Lamentations does, were not composed at the time of the city's destruction, but at least fifty years afterward, in conjunction with the rebuilding of its temple.[65]

2. In his discussion of the literary reaction to destruction in rabbinic literature, Shaye Cohen observes that the loss of three major wars—the great revolt, including the destruction of the Second Temple, in 66–70 C.E.; the uprising of the Jews in Cyrenaica, Egypt, and Cyprus in 115–117 C.E.; and the Bar Kokhba rebellion in 132–135 C.E.—provoked no literary reaction in Tannaitic times (70–200 C.E.). The silence was broken only in the Amoraic period (200–400 C.E.), and literary activity about the destruction continued into the post-Amoraic period (400–700 C.E.). Only at a safe distance from the events, suggests Cohen, could the rabbis recount stories about these events and sermonize about their meaning.[66]

3. Closer to our own day, many laments for the Holocaust, and in fact most Holocaust literature, postdate the event by at least thirty years and often longer, and were not written exclusively by survivors. Even the work of survivors is not all contemporaneous with the events. Trauma takes time to find literary expression.[67] Given these examples of the later composition of other literatures of destruction, we need not, and perhaps should not, date Lamentations to the period immediately following 586 B.C.E.

Another avenue to approach the question of dating is to estimate a date relative to other books of the Bible. There are clear affinities between Lamentations and both Jeremiah and Ezekiel. Julie Galambush has perceptively noted that both Lamentations and Ezekiel tend toward graphic descriptions. In both,

---

64. A wide range of dates for the individual poems and for the book as a whole has been proposed. See Provan, 10–11, for a quick summary. But most scholars date the book to shortly after the destruction of Jerusalem.

65. W. W. Hallo, "Lamentations and Prayers in Sumer and Akkad," in *Civilizations of the Ancient Near East,* ed. J. Sasson (4 vols.; New York: Charles Scribner's Sons, 1995), 3:1872.

66. S. Cohen, "The Destruction: From Scripture to Midrash," 18–19.

67. See also Moore, "Human Suffering," 537.

passersby are astonished at the place once called "perfect in beauty" (Lam 2:15; Ezek 16:14); foreigners have been admitted to the temple (Lam 1:10; Ezek 44:7); Jerusalem is compared with a *niddâ* (Lam 1:17; Ezek 36:17).[68]

The prophetic activity of Jeremiah and Ezekiel has been dated to 586–571 B.C.E., with the compilation of their books presumably not too much later. Lamentations could be seen as having emerged during the same period. If Lamentations drew on the discourse of these prophets (a question that needs further study), a date later than 571 would be reasonable.

It seems clear that Lamentations also knows something of the Deuteronomic and Priestly sources of the Torah, especially in regard to the paradigms of purity and politics, but there has been no study of this relationship. The dating of D and P is embroiled in controversy, which only adds to the difficulty of using them to date Lamentations.

The dependence of Second Isaiah on Lamentations is well known.[69] Second Isaiah, usually dated 550–538, would seem, therefore, to provide a terminus ad quem for Lamentations. But on the nature and extent of the Isaianic use of Lamentations there are differences of opinion. Benjamin Sommer finds relatively few allusions to Lamentations in Isaiah, and no allusions to Lam 5, prompting him to say that Second Isaiah did not know this chapter.[70] On the other hand, Patricia Willey (using different criteria) finds many more references to Lamentations, including Lam 5[71] F. W. Dobbs-Allsopp is reluctant to accept that Isaiah drew on Lamentations, since he is not confident that we can ascertain the direction of influence.[72] I am persuaded by Sommer and Willey that Second Isaiah is indeed drawing on the text of Lamentations, at least chapters 1–4. In terms of dating, this would place Lamentations before 538 B.C.E., the latest that Second Isaiah is generally dated.

The most reliable method for dating a book is by linguistic evidence, and Dobbs-Allsopp ("Linguistic Evidence") has provided an excellent study of it. Following the method of Avi Hurvitz, Robert Polzin, and others, Dobbs-Allsopp examines the vocabulary, certain syntactic usages, orthography, and the presence of Aramaisms. He concludes that the language of Lamentations has at least seventeen features typical of Late Biblical Hebrew, making the book

68. Galambush, *Jerusalem in the Book of Ezekiel*, 20.

69. Gottwald, *Studies*, 44–46; Westermann, 104–5; Willey, *Remember the Former Things*, 125–32 and passim; Sommer, *A Prophet Reads Scripture*, 127–30; Newsom, "Response to Gottwald."

70. Sommer, *Prophet Reads Scripture*, 130.

71. For Lam 5 see Willey, *Remember the Former Things*, 233–38.

72. "Linguistic Evidence," 8–9. See also Provan, 12. Dobbs-Allsopp explains the similarities in the two books by the fact that (according to his thesis) city laments were known in Israel for two hundred years before either of them, and therefore both Lamentations and Isaiah may be drawing on standard motifs and language.

clearly postexilic. On the other hand, the number of late features is not as large as books like Qoheleth, Esther, Ezra-Nehemiah, or Chronicles, so the late Persian or Maccabean period is ruled out. The language of the book falls, statistically speaking, in the transitional stage of Hebrew, like Ezekiel and Jonah, both of which are probably to be dated to the sixth century. In fact, Dobbs-Allsopp finds the linguistic profile of Lamentation to be closest to that of Ezekiel (compiled at some point after 571 B.C.E.). All the evidence combined points to a date in the sixth century, possibly as late as 520 but probably not later than about 540.[73] The book was written, not during or immediately after the destruction of Jerusalem, but during the exilic period, possibly near or at its end. As to where the book was written, that is impossible to say.

The real puzzle of Lamentations is not when it was written but why. Was its purpose liturgical? Was it written for public recitation to commemorate the destruction of the temple and Jerusalem? When and where did such commemorations begin to be celebrated? We have evidence for the use of Lamentations in rabbinic times, after the destruction of the Second Temple, but evidence for earlier periods is slimmer. Jeremiah 41:5 records that in the time of Gedaliah, that is, shortly after the fall of Jerusalem, eighty men came from Shechem, Shiloh, and Samaria (the former northern kingdom of Israel) with their beards shaved, their garments torn, and gashes on their bodies. In this state of mourning the men were bringing offerings to the "house of the Lord." These men may be among the first "mourners for Zion," as Isa 61:3 later refers to them, but even the Isaiah passage sheds little light on the practice of mourning for the temple in the exilic period. Somewhat more enlightening is Zech 7:5, with its mention of fast days (cf. Zech 8:19) and lament (*sāpôd*) in commemoration of the First Temple, proof that mourning for the temple had been institutionalized. But we do not know if the book of Lamentations or any of its chapters were part of the lamenting. We cannot prove that the book of Lamentations played any role in the commemoration until after the Second Temple had been destroyed.

It is tempting to draw an analogy from the Sumerian city laments, which were composed for recitation when the city's temple was being rebuilt. Indeed, it has been suggested that Lamentations was written on the occasion of the rebuilding of the temple.[74] But we should not jump to this conclusion, for, as Dobbs-Allsopp has noted, unlike the Sumerian laments, the biblical book makes no mention that God has returned to his city or that the temple has been rebuilt.[75] The date of the building of the Second Temple, ca. 515 B.C.E., would be at the late end of the range suggested by the other evidence for dating Lamentations. Perhaps a better

---

73. Dobbs-Allsopp, "Linguistic Evidence," concludes that the range of dates is 587–520, before the writing of the postexilic prophetic books.

74. Gwaltney, "Biblical Book of Lamentations," 258.

75. "Linguistic Evidence," 9 n. 47.

analogy with the Mesopotamian materials than the city laments, which were not reused in later rituals, is the *balag* and *eršemma* compositions, which continued to be part of the cultic liturgy from the Old Babylonian period through the first millennium B.C.E. But here we are in the realm of conjecture, with no evidence except possible analogies. We cannot say why the poems in Lamentations were composed, or why they were collected together. It is clear that the book ultimately gained a liturgical place in the commemoration of the Second Temple, and it may well have played a similar role in commemorating the First Temple before and during the Second Temple period. Its liturgical use may be the reason that the book entered the canon, and is more obviously the reason for its current place-ment within the Jewish canon—among the Five Scrolls, all of which are recited liturgically on different occasions throughout the year.

## 8. Lamentations at Qumran

The text of Lamentations is fairly well preserved, although there are a few irreg-ularities in lexical or syntactic usage (1:14; 2:6; 3:22; 4:9). The ancient versions are useful as evidence of early interpretations, but they do not suggest that a text different from the MT in anything other than small details ever circulated.[76] Four fragments of the book of Lamentations have been found among the Dead Sea Scrolls: 3QLam (3Q3, DJD 3:95), 4QLam (4Q111), 5QLam[a] (5Q6, DJD 3:174–77), 5QLam[b] (5Q7, DJD 3:178–79). They are in Herodian script, dating from the first century B.C.E. 4QLam deviates from the MT in several places, and some of these readings are noted in the commentary when they are of interest for the interpretation of the MT.[77] In addition to partially preserved copies of the biblical book, quotations from Lamentations appear in several nonbiblical poems from Qumran (most notably, 4Q179 and 4Q501; see also 4Q282 [for-merly 4Q241], 4Q439, 4Q445, 4Q453). These scrolls provide ample evidence that Lamentations was regarded as "canonical" in the Qumran community. Although it is not known for sure, the assumption of many scholars is that the book and the poems that allude to it were recited liturgically, but the occasion remains uncertain. The destruction of the temple and literature pertaining to it may have had special meaning for the Qumran community, since the commu-nity was at odds with the Jerusalem temple of its own day and felt itself to be still in exile. This feeling is reflected in the way that the noncanonical poems allude to Lamentations. These allusions, which are usually less than a verse in

---

76. For textual studies see W. Rudolph, "Der Text der Klagelieder," *ZAW* 56 (1938): 101–22; Albrektson, *Studies*; and Gottlieb, *Study*.

77. See F. M. Cross, "Studies in the Structure of Hebrew Verse: The Prosody of Lamentations 1:1–22," in *The Word of the Lord Shall Go Forth: Essays in Honor of David Noel Freedman*, ed. C. Meyers and M. O'Connor (Winona Lake, Ind.: Eisenbrauns, 1983), 129–55. Hillers (1992), 47–48, presents a collation of the MT and 4QLam readings (they are all from chap. 1).

length, do not follow the order of the biblical text and are widely interspersed throughout the poems. The allusions are not attempts to modernize the biblical language or provide interpretations per se, as Hillers (44) implies. Rather, they are artistic uses of scriptural phrases, purposely taken out of their original contexts and placed in new contexts in order to make a point.[78] These Qumran poems do not show us the text of Lamentations in the making; they show us the text as a vehicle for propaganda.

---

78. See A. Berlin, "Qumran Laments and the Study of Lament Literature," *Proceedings of the Fifth International Symposium of the Orion Center for the Study of the Dead Sea Scrolls.* Forthcoming.

# TRANSLATION
# AND COMMENTARY

# Lamentations 1:1–22
## Mourning and Shame

א
**1**   Alas, she sits alone,
      the city once thronged with people,[a]
      she has become like a widow.
   Noble among nations,[b]
      princess among provinces;
      she has become a forced laborer.

ב
**2**   Bitterly she sobs at night,
      with tears on her cheeks.
   There is no comforter for her
      from among all who love her.
   All her friends have betrayed her,
      have become her enemies.

ג
**3**   Judah was exiled after[c] misery
      and much servitude;
   she dwells among the nations,
      finds no resting place.
   All her pursuers have trapped her
      in narrow straits.

ד
**4**   Zion's roads are in mourning,
      empty of festival[d] pilgrims;
      all her gates are desolate.
   Her priests are groaning,
      her maidens are grieving,[e]
      and she—it is bitter for her.

ה
**5**   Her foes have become the master,
      her enemies rest easy,
   for the Lord made her suffer
      for her many transgressions.

Her little children have gone away as captives[f]
    before the foe.


ו
**6**    Gone from Dear Zion
        is all her splendor.
    Her princes have become like stags[g]
        that find no pasture,
    but go on exhausted
        before the pursuer.


ז
**7**    Jerusalem remembered
            (in) the days of her misery and her trouble,[h]
        all her treasures[i] of earlier days.
    When her people fell into the hand of the foe,
        and there was no one to help her,
        foes saw her, mocked her collapse.[j]


ח
**8**    Grievously has Jerusalem sinned,
            therefore has she been banished.[k]
    All who once respected her treat her as worthless,
        for they have seen her nakedness.
    Indeed, she herself groans,
        and turns away.


ט
**9**    Her impurity is in her skirts,
            she had no regard for her future;
    and she had come down amazingly,
            there is no comforter for her.
    "Look, LORD, upon my misery,
            for the enemy is triumphant."[l]


י
**10**    The foe spread his hand
            over all her treasures.
    Indeed, she has seen the nations
            enter her temple,
    concerning whom you had commanded:
            "They shall not enter your assembly."

כ
**11** All her people are groaning,
    searching for bread;
they gave their treasures for food
    to sustain life.
Look, LORD, and see
    what a beggar[m] I have become.

ל
**12** May it not happen to you, all you passersby.
    Look, see:
Is there any pain like my pain,
    which befell me,
which the LORD made me suffer
    on the day of his anger?

מ
**13** From on high he sent fire into my bones,
    and he brought it down.[n]
He spread a net for my feet,
    he held me back.
He made me desolate,
    all day long languishing.

נ
**14** My yoke of transgressions was fashioned,[o]
    with his hand they were entwined,
they mounted upon my neck,
    it sapped my strength.
My LORD gave me into the hands
    of those I cannot withstand.

ס
**15** He trampled[p] all my warriors,
    the LORD in my midst.
He proclaimed against me a set time
    to crush my youths.
The LORD trod the winepress
    of Dear Maiden Judah.

ע
**16**  For these things do I sob,
           my eyes, my eyes flow with water.
        For far from me is any comforter,
           anyone to keep me alive.
        My children are desolate,
           for the enemy has prevailed.

פ
**17**  Zion spread out her hands,
           there is no comforter for her.
        The LORD has commanded for Jacob^q
           that those around him^r are his foes.
        Jerusalem has become
           a menstruating woman among them.^s

צ
**18**  The LORD is in the right,
           for I have rebelled against his mouth.
        Listen well, all you peoples,
           and see my pain.
        My maidens and youths
           have gone into captivity.

ק
**19**  I called to my lovers,
           they deceived me.
        My priests and elders
           expired in the city
        as they searched for food
           to sustain^t their life.

ר
**20**  See, LORD, how distressed I am,
           my bowels churn,
        my heart is turned over inside me,
           how very bitter I am.^u
        Outside the sword bereaved,
           inside—death.^v

ש
**21**  They heard that I was groaning,
           "There is no comforter for me."

All my enemies who heard my distress
    rejoiced that you had caused it.
O bring the day you proclaimed,
    and let them be like me.

ה

**22**  Let their evildoing come before you,
    and do to them
what you did to me
    for all my transgressions.
For many are my groans,
    and my heart is languishing.

a. The word *rabbātî* occurs twice in this verse, but unlike most exegetes I have construed it differently in each case because the grammatical construction is different (cf. Schramm, "Poetic Patterning," 180). Here, *rabbātî ʿām* is a construct chain, meaning "having much/many people," hence "full, thronged." Cf. 1 Sam 2:5, *rabbat bānîm*.

b. In the phrase *rabbātî baggôyim*, *rabbātî* is an independent noun followed by a preposition. The term *rab* is a title, "chief," a feminine equivalent of *rab* in expressions like *rab hāḥōbēl* (Jonah 1:6), *rab sārîs* (2 Kgs 18:17). *Rbty* and *śrty* are synonyms, interchangeable in such expressions as *rab ṭabbāḥîm* (2 Kgs 25:8) and *śar haṭṭabbāḥîm* (Gen 37:36). In Ugaritic the pair *rbt* and *trrt* are used in connection with cities and as epithets of deities. See Jonas C. Greenfield, "The Epithets *rbt // trrt* in the *KRT* Epic," in *Perspectives on Language and Text: Essays and Poems in Honor of Francis I. Andersen*, ed. E. W. Conrad and E. G. Newing (Winona Lake, Ind.: Eisenbrauns, 1987), 35–37. See also McDaniel, "Philological Studies, I," 29–31. Unlike McDaniel, I do not take *rbty* and *śrty* as formal epithets of the city, but rather as personifications.

c. The meaning of the prepositional *mêm* before *ʿŏnî* and *ʿăbōdâ* is problematic. Gordis interprets it as the "*mêm* of condition" ("exiled in a state of misery"), but his other examples of this *mêm* in the Bible are not convincing. I follow Hillers, who understands it in a temporal sense, "after." Thus, from a state of misery and servitude, that is, being a vassal to Babylonia, Judah has gone to a worse state, exile. Linafelt, *Surviving Lamentations*, 159 n. 13, prefers to take the *mêm* "in the plain sense of the particle" and understands "from suffering and much toil" as the situation in Jerusalem.

d. Hebrew *môʿēd* is best rendered here as "festival." The word occurs in 2:6 as "assembly" or possibly even "appointed place = temple."

e. I follow Hillers, Provan, and many recent translations (so also Rashi) in taking *nûgôf* as the *nipʿal* participle of *yāgâ*—cf. Lam 1:5, 12; 3:32, 33. The nouns *yāgôn* and *nāḥâ* occur together several times (Isa 35:10; 51:11; Ps 31:11). According to Anderson, *nh* may denote an activity that is publicly visible, and that is often associated with lamentations (*Time to Mourn*, 70). LXX has "led away," apparently from *nhg*. To be sure, *nwgwt* in the *niphʿal* is unusual (found only in the unintelligible Zeph 3:18); however, I am not persuaded that the MT should be emended to *nipʿal*, or, as F. M. Cross, "Studies in the Structure of Hebrew Verse," 138, has recently suggested, that the MT is a shortened form of *nĕhûgôt*.

f. The normal construction of the phrase "to go into captivity" (*hālak baššebî*) has the preposition *b-* before *šĕbî*, as in Amos 9:4 ("if you go into captivity before your enemies"); Isa 46:2; Jer 20:6; etc. Since *b-* is absent here, *šĕbî* is best taken as an adverbial accusative. See Waltke and O'Connor, *Biblical Hebrew Syntax,* 169–77.

g. Pham (*Mourning,* 44) prefers "rams," reading *ʾêlîm,* following the LXX and Vulgate, since "rams" is a title for leaders in Exod 15:14 and elsewhere.

h. To be consistent with the rest of the context, v. 7 must refer to Jerusalem's remembering the time of the siege and destruction. The problem is that the Hebrew text lacks the particle "in" before "the days," although it is supplied in many translations. If "in" is not supplied, the verse seems to mean that Jerusalem remembers the days of her misery. That in turn makes "all her treasures of earlier days" seem out of place and unintelligible. Some commentators therefore omit this phrase altogether. 4QLam reads *zkrh yhwh mrwdyh ʾšr mymy qdm,* "Remember, YHWH, her troubles that are from the days of old," but this only adds to the confusion.

Hebrew *mĕrûdêhā,* "her trouble," is a rare word (cf. Lam 3:19 and Isa 58:7, where it also occurs in collocation with *ʿanĕyî,* "misery"). It may derive either from the root *rdh* or from *mrd.* The meaning "homeless" (*HALOT* 2:633) seems to be based on the context of Isa 58:7.

i. "Her treasures," *maḥămudêhā,* occurs also in 1:10, 11; 2:4. It is generally rendered "pleasures" in our verse—that is, happy times or experiences. Indeed, its sense is things that delight her, treasured moments or treasured memories.

j. The word *mišbattehā* is most likely from *šbt,* "to cease, end," but perhaps also echoes of *šby,* "captivity." 4QLam reads *mšbrh,* "her ruins."

k. The word *nîdâ* has an unusual form, but it is probably from *nwd.* 4QLam reads *lnwd.* The meaning "menstruant," *niddâ,* is not supported by the orthography. See the commentary.

l. The expression *higdîl ʾoyēb* means the enemy boasts about its superiority.

m. The word *zôlēlâ* is usually taken from the root *zwl,* with the sense of "lacking value." V. A. Hurowitz, "*zllh* = Peddler/Tramp/Vagabond/Beggar: Lamentations 1:11 in Light of Akkadian *zilulû,*" *VT* 59 (1999): 542–45, has connected the word with Akkadian *zilulû,* "tramp, vagabond, beggar." 4QLamᵃ reads *zwll.*

n. God is the subject of all the verbs in the verse. The word *wayyirdennâ* may be construed from the root *rdh,* "to rule over," or from *yrd,* "to descend." The form in the MT, *yireddennâ,* indicates *rdh,* "he ruled over her/it." Many translations emend to *yōreddennâ,* "he caused it to come down," and I have followed them. The third-person feminine singular suffix seems to have no appropriate antecedent. Ibn Ezra takes "fire" as the antecedent and understands the meaning to be that God ruled (*rdh*) over the fire. Similarly, Provan, 49. The Syriac and Vulgate have a first-person pronoun, which parallels the surrounding phrases.

o. The word *niśqad* occurs nowhere else in the Bible and has been the subject of much conjecture. A common variant is *nšqd,* "to keep watch," which occurs in some Hebrew manuscripts and was the basis of some ancient translations (see Provan, 50). I have chosen a neutral word to convey that a yoke is being made.

p. The word *sillâ,* from the root *slh,* close to *sll,* literally means "heap up." Hillers translates it literally, and equates it with a harvest image. But *sll* is often used of the earthen ramp in sieges, prepared by stamping down earth around the city wall. It is this stamping down, I think, that is the intended image here, and what the Peshitta may have had in mind in its rendering *kbaš*. (Several manuscripts of the Targum also read *kbś*.) RSV and others who translate "despised" or "flouted" take the verb from *slh*, as in Ps 119:118 (in the *qal*).

q. The phrase is difficult. Cross, "Studies," 147, prefers the reading in 4QLam, *sph* for MT's *ṣwh*, with the meaning "The LORD kept watch on Jacob: his enemies have surrounded him." But this reading is at best a marginal improvement.

r. Heb. *sābîb* means "neighbors," as in Pss 44:14; 76:12; 89:8, and is so translated in NIV and NRSV.

s. 4QLam reads *lndwḥ* for *lĕniddâ* and *ṣph* ("kept watch") for *ṣwh*. Neither reading is helpful.

t. A jussive following an indicative. See Paul Joüon, *A Grammar of Biblical Hebrew*; translated and revised by T. Muraoka. Rome: Pontifical Biblical Institute, 1993, §116e.

u. The phrase *kî mārô mārîtî* is generally taken to mean "for I have indeed rebelled," but the admission of fault is not congruent with the expression of emotion in the rest of the verse. I follow the suggestion of C. L. Seow, "A Textual Note on Lamentations 1:20," *CBQ* 47 (1985): 416–19, that the meaning is "how very bitter I am" from the root *mrr* rather than from the root *mrh/mry*, "to rebel." But note that *mārîtî* occurs in v. 18, where it clearly means "I rebelled."

v. Many interpreters have found the particle *k-* in *kammāwet* problematic. Taking it as "like death" forces the sense to be something less than death but similar to it—e.g., great suffering. This weakens the force of the phrase and goes against the common trope of describing death inside and outside the city. Gordis interprets the *kāp* as asseverative (also in 5:3); that is, an emphatic particle. I find this the best interpretation. See Waltke and O'Connor, *Biblical Hebrew Syntax*, 203–4.

## Commentary

Shame, mourning, and suffering are the themes that dominate chapter 1. Jerusalem is shamed by her destruction, in her own eyes and for all the world to see, for her punishment reveals the magnitude of her sin. Jerusalem is a guilty victim, and guilt leads to shame. But her guilt and shame are offset by her suffering, and this suffering drowns out all other thoughts. Jerusalem is in a state of utter wretchedness, unable to bear the pain of her punishment.

The personification of a city as a woman is a common image in prophetic literature, with possible antecedents in Mesopotamian literature and successors in Greek literature—but nowhere is it developed more effectively than in the personification of Jerusalem in this chapter. Here a kaleidoscope of images turns quickly from a lonely widow, to a degraded princess, to a whore, to a rape victim, to a betrayed lover, to an abandoned wife. The woman betrayed by her lovers is the country betrayed by its allies; the mother mourning the loss of her children is the city lamenting the exile of her citizens; the sexual violation of the woman-city is the religious violation of the temple precincts; the sexual sin of immorality is the religious sin of idolatry. This last equation, immorality =

idolatry, lies beneath the images of the harlot and of the unfaithful wife, in their many permutations. The poem moves back and forth from the woman to the city in such a way that the figurative and the literal blend together.

The image of the city-woman in her abject state elicits both revulsion and pity. As we watch her, and the poet forces us to watch her, we are torn by ambivalent urges: we cannot bear to look but we cannot turn our eyes away. The more we look, the more we shame her by seeing that which should not be seen. But we must look, for the poet calls upon us to see what has happened to the city and to partake in her suffering. We become actors in the "drama" of this chapter. This chapter is a poetic reenactment of the rites of mourning, and we become mourners along with Jerusalem.[1] Over and over we hear the sounds and see the signs of mourning: the widowed city sobs, her eyes flow with tears, her roads are in mourning, her priests groan, her maidens grieve. Yet, with all this mourning, there is no comforter (vv. 2, 9, 16, 17, 21). The ritualized mourning of the ancient Near East requires a comforter, but in our chapter the role of comforter is not filled, suggesting that the process of mourning cannot be completed; the mourning is infinite.

The chapter is a plea for comfort in the face of the absence of a comforter. According to Gary Anderson, one of the definitions of "comfort," in its technical, ritualized sense, is "assuming the state of mourning alongside the mourner."[2] This is what the poem demands its readers do. The poet and the readers mourn with Jerusalem, thereby filling the role of the missing comforters, as they participate in the unending mourning for the city. In another sense, though, the state of mourning is permanent, for without the temple there can be no joy, only its antithesis, mourning (see the Introduction, Mourning as a Religious Concept, and the commentary on v. 4). God is the ultimate comforter, as Jeremiah (31:13) and Second Isaiah (Isa 51:12; 52:9) envision,[3] and only he can fill this role. In this context we can say that Lam 1, and perhaps the entire book, is a call to God to be Zion's comforter.

The scene of mourning is conveyed through two speaking voices, two perspectives, united in their understanding of the condition of the city and its people. The third-person voice of an observer describes Jerusalem (vv. 1–11), and then the first-person voice of Jerusalem herself speaks (vv. 12–22), reinforcing the picture in more graphic terms and with more immediacy. Yet these two parts of the chapter are not completely separate, for each voice intrudes on the other. The observer lets us hear Jerusalem's words in v. 9, and Jerusalem's speech is interrupted in v. 17 by the voice of the observer. There are other observers within the poem as well—the passersby (v. 12) and the mocking enemy (v. 7)—who

---

1. Pham, *Mourning*, 15–35 and passim, drawing on Anderson, *Time to Mourn,*, 49–53, 84–87 and passim, emphasizes the role that mourning rites play in Lam 1–2.

2. *Time to Mourn*, 84.

3. See Willey, *Remember*, 156.

serve as further witnesses to Jerusalem's degradation. God is the witness whom the poem seeks to provoke. He who caused the destruction must now see how much misery it has wrought and must bring it to an end. But God's only response is silence.

[1:1–11] These verses are a portrait of Jerusalem, destroyed, shamed, and dejected. The picture opens with the unnamed city, sitting empty and alone, in contrast to the thriving metropolis she once was. The image of the city as widow leads to the idea of mourning and abandonment, and it evokes pity. But almost immediately a different set of associations impinges: this apparently pitiful woman had taken lovers, she had acted immorally, and she deserved her punishment. These ideas are not contradictory, but they generate a cognitive and emotional tension that is in play throughout the chapter.

[1–2] The lonely widow laments but finds no comfort. The first word of the chapter, *'êkâ*, signals the discourse of lament, as it does also in chapters 2 and 4. It is an exclamation of despair that marks a sudden change from a glorious past to the degraded present (cf. Isa 1:21; Jer 48:17; Ezek 26:17), and the nature of that change is described in the rest of v. 1. The *pāsēq* in the MT after *'êkâ*, indicating a slight pause, suggests that the word stands slightly apart from what follows it. In that sense, *'êkâ* introduces the chapter as a whole.

I follow the accentuation of the MT, which puts the major break in the verse after "widow." This yields two groups of three lines (see also Provan, 36), a somewhat different pattern from most of the other verses, and from the rendering of this verse in most recent translations (NRSV, NJPS). The division into two groups of lines corresponds to the two parallel comparisons between Jerusalem's past and her present. She was once a flourishing metropolis and now stands deserted; and she was once the capital of an independent country and is now the captive bound to provide forced labor for the conqueror.

The idea of loneliness and vulnerability is nicely encapsulated in the image of the widow, the bereaved woman without a male protector who, like the orphan, the poor, and the stranger, is accorded special protection in biblical law. The term is used metaphorically also in Isa 47:8 (where it is the opposite of "dwelling secure") and Isa 54:4. Beyond signaling loneliness, in v. 1 it carries the additional implication that Jerusalem has lost her "husband," that is, that God's presence has departed. The widow image may also have a political implication that makes the two parts of v. 1 more closely related than first meets the eye. On the Merneptah Stele, line 27, the Egyptian word for "widow" is used to describe plundered enemy lands. When applied to cities, the term "widow" refers to a once independent city that has become a vassal.[4] In the poetic parallelism in v. 1, this idea is given more concrete expression, for the vassal-widow is also the corvée laborer.

4. C. Cohen, "The 'Widowed' City."

The image of the widowed city is joined by the image of the city as a mother who has lost her children. The "mother" city, once *rabbātî ʿām*, "thronged with people" (which recalls *rabbat bānîm*, "having many children," of 1 Sam 2:5), is now empty both on the inside (gone are the bustling crowds at the gates, royal courts, and temple) and on the outside (for the villages of Judah in the surrounding countryside have been ravaged by war and now lie desolate). The empty city sits alone (*yāšbâ bādād* or *šakēn bādād*), a phrase that has both positive and negative connotations. On the one hand, a city or people dwelling alone is secure, unmolested by enemies, protected by God (Num 23:9; Deut 33:28; Jer 49:31). On the other hand, dwelling alone may signify exclusion, isolation (Isa 27:10; Jer 15:17; Mic 7:14). Here the connotation is negative: the city is empty of her inhabitants and alone with no one to help her.

If loneliness was the primary connotation of the "widow" in v. 1, it is mourning in v. 2. She sobs "at night," the saddest time of day, when one is alone and can vent one's feelings (cf. Ps 6:7). Her sobbing is not silent (the root *bkh* means "cry aloud, utter the sound of sobbing"), so others can hear her; but contrary to expectation, those who hear her, those who care about her, do not come to comfort her.

The term *ʾōhăbêhā*, "all those who love her," means her associates or supporters and is in the same semantic range as "brother" and "friend" (Ps 88:19; Prov 17:17; 18:24). It is the opposite of "enemy" (Prov 27:6). An *ʾōhēb* rejoices with someone in good times and mourns with him in times of trouble (Isa 66:10). By extension, *ʾōhēb* means "ally" in a political sense.[5] It is taken by most commentators in that sense here, referring to the other nations with which Judah allied herself but which did not come to her defense. A nation was obligated to mourn the loss of an ally, and to provide comfort to his survivors.[6] The term takes on yet another connotation here, according to many exegetes, because "love" is used in reference to the relationship between God and Israel, and because the prophets condemned foreign alliances as showing lack of faith in God.[7] So "her lovers" and "her friends" hint at Judah's unfaithfulness, mentioned more overtly in v. 19 (where the term "lovers," *mě ʾahăbay*, occurs). As Hillers points out, the verse evokes both sympathy and condemnation: sympathy for the sufferer abandoned by friends (a known motif in laments—cf. Pss 88:19; 38:12; and the Babylonian Poem of the Righteous Sufferer I, 84–88 [*ANET*, 596]); and a sense that this sufferer deserved her loneliness because she was unfaithful. The double entendre is echoed in the verb *bgd*, "betray, act treacherously," which is used for infidelity in marriage (Jer 3:20), the treachery

5. 1 Kgs 5:15; perhaps 1 Sam 18:16; see W. Moran, "The Ancient Near Eastern Background of the Love of God in Deuteronomy," *CBQ* 25 (1963): 77–87.

6. Cf. 2 Sam 10:1–2 = 1 Chr 19:1; and P. Artzi, "Mourning in International Relations," in *Death in Mesopotamia*, 161–70.

7. J. A. Thompson, "Israel's 'Lovers.'"

of family and friends (Job 6:15), and the dissolving of political or social relationships (Judg 9:23). For this reason, several translations (NIV, NRSV) render the word "her lovers," emphasizing the city's sexual sin, a rendering to which Provan takes exception because he does not see a mention of sin before v. 5; in v. 2 we have only Jerusalem's loneliness and lack of comfort. His point is reflected in my translation, though I do not exclude the multilayeredness of all these associations. On first encountering the word, however, the primary association is with friends or allies who are supposed to render comfort but do not. Gradually, as the poem advances, we may read back into v. 2 the notion of lovers, though it is not strictly necessary. The idea that mourning and comfort are denied to Jerusalem because of her sin is found in Jer 16:5–7, where it is not the lovers (other nations) who fail to mourn, but rather the prophet who is forbidden to mourn because God is punishing the people for their sins of idolatry. So, too, in Lamentations Jerusalem has no one to mourn for her, except the poet who, in lamenting the absence of mourning, acts as a mourner.

[3–4] The camera, focused till now on the city-woman, gives us a shot of the people who have been exiled and then of the place they left behind. The "misery and servitude," *mē ʿŏnî* and *ʿăbōdâ* (perhaps a hendiadys, "miserable servitude"), that the Judeans experienced has no clear referent. The terms occur several times in collocation, notably in Gen 15:13; Exod 1:11; and Deut 26:6, where the reference is to the enslavement in Egypt.[8] The terms, then, can be seen as an allusion to the enslavement in Egypt, an allusion further reinforced at the end of v. 3 by *mĕṣārîm*, "narrow straits," a word that sounds like *miṣrayim*, "Egypt." Compare a similar reference to Egypt in Hos 8:13: "Now he will remember your sin and note your transgression; they will return to Egypt." The vassalage of Judah to Babylonia is likened to the enslavement in Egypt in that it returned the people to their preexodus state. But unlike the Egyptian experience, the servitude to Babylonia led not to freedom but to exile. Later, the postexilic prophets will compare the return from exile to the exodus.[9]

The idea of exile is further expressed in the phrase "she dwells among the nations." While some exegetes take this phrase as describing the preexilic situation, I understand it as referring to conditions after the exile, where "she finds no resting place" (cf. Rashi and NRSV). Provan notes the contrast between Jerusalem sitting alone (*bdd*) while her people now dwell amid other nations. This contrast brings to mind other verses containing *bdd*, which convey the

---

8. A. Frisch, "*wʿnytm* (I Reg 12,7): An Ambiguity and Its Function in the Context," *ZAW* 103 (1991): 415–18.

9. In an excursus to chap. 1 in his commentary on Lamentations, Dobbs-Allsopp also identifies the allusion to Egyptian servitude in the words "misery" and "much servitude." He extends the reference to Egypt to other verses in the chapter that mention *ʾnḥ*, "groan," and the idea of Israel crying out to the Lord and the Lord hearing their cries and remembering them (cf. Exod 2:23–24).

opposite of "dwelling among the nations." The most famous is Num 23:9: "a people dwelling alone/secure, not reckoned among the nations." Cf. also Deut 33:28. Hence for Judah to dwell alone, apart from the nations, may have been the ideal that has now been lost.

The phrase "finds no resting place" clearly echoes Deut 28:64–65, also a description of dispersion: "The LORD will scatter you among all the peoples. . . . And among those nations you will not find respite, and there will be no resting place for your feet." Note that Lam 1:5 is also informed by Deut 28, further evidence that the verse refers to Judah's state of exile. The connotation of "finding a resting place" is to find a place to establish a new home, as in the case of Noah's dove (Gen 8:9) and in Ruth 3:1, where Naomi seeks a "resting place" for Ruth, meaning a husband and a new family. Judah has lost its old home and will not find a new one.

Verse 4 shows a picture of this lost home. The city's roads and gates, normally crowded and noisy with travelers, are now empty and silent, and are personified as mourners just like the city. The context of mourning may also explain the mention of the priests and maidens (*bĕtûlôt*), which at first seems like an odd combination. Women, specifically *bĕtûlôt*, were public singers or mourners (Jer 31:13; Lam 2:10), and both women and priests are found in the context of mourning in Joel 1:8–9.[10] Here the priests and the maidens now act as mourners, rather than in their usual festival manner, extending and concretizing the image of Zion in mourning. In Isaiah's prophecy of the return of the exiles (Isa 35:10 = 51:11), the "groaning and grieving" here associated with the mourners will disappear, replaced by gladness and joy. Joy and mourning should not be understood simply as expressions of emotion, but, as Gary Anderson makes clear, they are religious concepts.[11] Joy is associated with sacrifice and being in God's presence, while mourning is associated with being cut off from God. The mourning of Zion's roads, priests, and maidens is, then, more than a poetic metaphor. In the conceptual world of the Israelite cult, mourning signifies the absence of festival sacrifices and their accompanying celebrations.

[5] In contrast to the people of Judah, the enemy enjoys security and delights in Jerusalem's suffering. The reference to "her foes have become her master," literally "the head," evokes the curse in Deut 28:44: "he will be the head and you will be the tail." (Cf. Deut 28:13.) The enemy rests easy (*šālēm*, "be calm, feel secure, be at peace") now that they have won, for there is no need to maintain a state of war. Compare Ps 122:6, where *šaʾălû* parallels *šālôm*. By contrast, Judah is pursued and without a place to rest. Deuteronomy 28:41 is also the source for

---

10. Hillers notes that in the Ugaritic epic tradition, Anat, called *btlt*, is the principal mourner. See Hillers, 82–84. On women as performers see S. D. Goitein, *ʿIyyunim bammiqra* (Studies in Scripture) (Tel Aviv: Yavneh, 1957), 248–82 (= "Women as Creators of Biblical Genres," *Prooftexts* 8 [1988]: 1–33).

11. *Time to Mourn,*, 70 and passim.

the idea of children going into captivity, but instead of Deuteronomy's "sons and daughters," our verse uses the more emotionally laden term *ʿôlāl*, "little child."

Yet the credit for Judah's condition is not given to the enemies. It is the Lord who has made her suffer (*hip ʿil* of *yāgâ*), because of her rebellions. The word *pešaʿ*, "transgression," signifies a rebellion against an overlord, in a political sense (2 Kgs 1:1; 3:5), and also, in a religious sense, a rebellion against God. From the Babylonian point of view, Judah has rebelled against Babylonian overlordship and had to be vanquished. But Judean theology sees Judah's sin as a rebellion against God that had to be punished.

[6–11] The focus returns to the city—first her current low state (vv. 6–7), then her sin and degradation (vv. 8–10). This section ends with another view of the misery of the people (v. 11), and a transition to the second half of the chapter in which Jerusalem speaks.

[6–7] "Dear Zion," *bat-ṣiyyôn*, is a common epithet for Jerusalem (see Introduction, Excursus 1, for a discussion of this and similar epithets). The "splendor" may refer to the treasures of gold and silver, plundered by the enemy; or perhaps it refers to the city's leaders, described in the following lines as stags. Those who were once the leaders of the community are now driven out by the enemy like hunted animals, exhausted but unable to rest. Hillers (85) notes a stag image among the curses in a vassal treaty of Esarhaddon: "Just as a stag is chased and killed, so may your avengers chase and kill you, your brothers, your sons" (*ANET*, 540, lines 576–78).

[8–10] Jerusalem's sin is the cause of her exile, and her exile is the cause of her shame. Just as her sin is expressed in the sexual terms of unfaithfulness and adultery, so her shame is expressed in the sexual terms of nakedness (sexual disgrace) and sexual abuse. Seeing someone's nakedness was the height of indecency in the ancient world, and so the use of the term *ʿerwâ*, "nakedness," had a much more devastating effect on the ancient reader than it does on the modern one. Nakedness is used metaphorically in Isa 47:3 to disgrace Babylonia: "Your nakedness shall be uncovered and your shame shall be seen." It is also applied to a country in Gen 42:9, 12: "to see the nakedness of the land," meaning to see its weakness, to see what should not be seen. Worse than nakedness is the sexual abuse, even rape, that Jerusalem suffered at the hand of her enemy (v. 10). At this point, disgust for the immoral Jerusalem turns to sympathy for the abused city-woman, for no matter how grave her offense, the cruel treatment she received is more than she can bear.

[8] Jerusalem is the object of derision and shame. The word *nîdâ*, here translated as "banished," has provoked extensive comment because of its anomalous form. Three lines of interpretation can be found from medieval to modern times, all grammatically possible but equally difficult, and all supported by the immediate context. The first understands the root as *nwd* and is most probably correct. However, *nwd* has two meanings. One is "to move or shake [the head]" in

the sense of "to mock or deride" (Jer 18:16; Ps 44:15). The phrase would then mean that Jerusalem has become an object of derision. A second possibility is to take *nwd* as "wanderer." Both "derision" and "wanderer" are derived from the same root by *HALOT* and by Ibn Ezra. It is a matter of taste as to which an exegete prefers. LXX and Rashi favor "wanderer," while Ibn Ezra opts for "derision." I have chosen the idea of wandering because the consequence of sin is less likely to be derision and more likely to be banishment or exile. The root *nwd* recalls Cain (Gen 4:12–14), the prototype of the exiled person, who was banished for defiling the land with spilled blood. But, to be sure, the following phrase speaks of the lack of respect with which Jerusalem is treated, so "derision" may also be in play. A third interpretation takes the meaning to be "a menstruant" (and thereby in a state of ritual impurity). The orthography does not support this interpretation since *niddâ*, "a menstruant," from the root *ndd*, would be written with a double *dālet* and no *yôd* (see 1:17). But the mention of "nakedness" and "impurity" in the following lines may also evoke the word *niddâ* in a play on words with *nîdâ*. Leviticus 20:21 links *niddâ* and *ʿerwâ*, as does Ezek 22:10. It may be best to conclude that all three associations adhere to the word, and the dominant one shifts as we proceed from line to line—from the consequence of sin, to the scorn of others, to the idea of nakedness and impurity in her skirts.

**[9]** For many readers (especially those who take *nîdâ* in v. 8 as a menstruant) the reference to impurity in her skirts evokes the image of a menstruant. It must be pointed out, though, that a menstruant is ritually, but not morally, impure; menstruation is not a sin (see Introduction, The Paradigm of Purity). I must stress that this verse is not evidence that menstruation was considered morally offensive or disgusting. If the intended image is a menstruant, ritual impurity must be interpreted as a metaphor for the moral impurity of which Jerusalem was guilty by virtue of her unfaithfulness to God. If the phrase is interpreted as a menstruant metaphor, it may suggest that Jerusalem's moral impurity was obvious for all to see, as visible as a bloodstain on the skirt of a menstruating woman. But this interpretation seems forced. In fact, the verse is better understood as not referring to menstruation but to the impurity of sexual immorality.

Knowing that menstruation does not render a woman morally impure, Pham (*Mourning*, 75) is reluctant to see the image of a menstruant here. (She does not entertain the possibility of the metaphoric use of ritual impurity.) She suggests instead that the "filth" (her rendering of *ṭumʾâ*, "impurity") on the skirt refers to the fact that Jerusalem has been sitting on the ground as a mourner does, and is therefore dirty. I find nothing to support taking *ṭumʾâ* in this sense. But Pham does give a fine explication of *šûlêhā*, "her skirts," as the lower part of the garment, sometimes associated with one's modesty (*HALOT* 4:1442 gives the meaning in Lam 1:9 as "seams or lower part of the body" and in Jer 13:22, 26 and Nah 3:5 as "pubic area.") Nahum 3:5 and Jer 13:22, 26 speak of lifting up or stripping off the "skirts" and exposing the woman's nakedness. From the meaning and contexts of "skirts," it becomes clear that this term refers to sexual immodesty or impropriety, not to menstruation. The idea of a menstruant is not present at all in our verse. The phrase "her impurity is in her skirts" means that her impurity results from her sexual immorality. She is not a menstruant; she is a whore.

[10] Jerusalem's sexual misbehavior is followed by the enemy's treatment of her, described as a heinous sexual act. He molested her ("spread his hand") and he raped her (*bôʾ*, "enter," has sexual connotations). The image is both of a woman violated and of the desecration of holy objects and holy space. The words of Alan Mintz, cited in many commentaries, are worth quoting in full.

> The text here implies that in her glory Fair Zion conducted herself with easy virtue and "gave no thought to her end" (1:8), so that what began as unwitting, voluntary promiscuity, suddenly turned into unwished for, forcible defilement. The force of this image of violation is founded on the correspondence body // Temple and genitals // Inner Sanctuary. So far have things gone that even in the secret place of intimacy to which only the single sacred partner may be admitted, the enemy has thrust himself and "spread his hands over everything dear to her" (v. 10).[12]

The enemy who entered the holy precincts forbidden to him is not named, but by implication is equated with the most traditionally despised of Israel's enemies. "They shall not enter your assembly" is a reference to Deut 23:3–4: "An Ammonite or Moabite may not enter the assembly of the LORD." Not only are the Babylonians equated with Ammon and Moab, but their invasion of the temple is made to seem even more religiously reprehensible because it belies a divine command.

Dobbs-Allsopp adduced a Mesopotamian parallel to our passage in the description of the despoiling of a divine image in a Sumerian *balag*. It hints at the possible conceptual background that informs the biblical poet and at the same time shows how the Bible's more abstract view of God and more sophisticated use of metaphor transform this ancient Near Eastern background into a much more compelling image.

> That enemy entered my dwelling-place wearing his shoes
> That enemy laid his unwashed hands on me
> He laid his hands on me, he frightened me
> That enemy laid his hands on me, he prostrated me with fright
> I was afraid, he was not afraid (of me)
> He tore my garments off me, he dressed his wife (in them)
> That enemy cut off my pure lapis-lazuli, he placed it on his daughter.[13]

12. *Hurban*, 25.
13. *Weep*, 48.

**[11]** It is difficult to understand "treasures" in this verse as referring to the same "treasures" of v. 10, that is, the holy vessels of the temple. Here the term may refer to privately owned objects of value that could be exchanged for food. The verse would then allude to the inflated food prices during the time of famine. Compare 2 Kgs 6:25: "There was a great famine in Samaria, and the siege continued until a donkey's head sold for eighty shekels of silver and a quarter of a *kab* of doves' dung [carob pods] for five shekels." The phrase, however, becomes more moving if we take "treasures" as referring to human beings (cf. Ezek 24:16; Lam 2:4), in this case children, as in Hos 9:16. Many exegetes understand this to mean that the people bartered their children for food, in order to keep themselves alive. Hillers (88) notes a parallel in the Atra-hasis Epic that seems to view the sale of family members in a time of extended famine as the prelude to cannibalism.

> When the fifth year arrived,
> A daughter would eye her mother coming in;
> A mother would not even open her door to her daughter.
> A daughter would watch the scales (at the sale of her) mother,
> A mother would watch the scales (at the sale of her) daughter.
> When the sixth year arrived
> They served up a daughter for a meal,
> Served up a son for food.[14]

The difficulty I have with this interpretation is that in a besieged city, human beings had little value as a commodity to be sold. In normal times, adults and children were sold as slaves, but what use was there for slaves during a siege? There was little work for them to do and they still had to be fed. I propose a slightly different interpretation. In times of siege famines, parents would sell their children cheaply or even give them away (the verb in our verse is *ntn*, "give," not "barter," as numerous translations have) to someone who would feed them in exchange for their labor—in order to keep *the children* alive.[15] It is not that the parents are making a profit from the sale of their children in order to buy food. Rather the desperate parents, who can no longer feed their children, are forced to give them away for the good of the children. While not the usual way of interpreting the verse, the words can support this interpretation. The idiom *hāšîb nepeš* here and in v. 19 means "to sustain life" in the sense of providing nourishment, but here, unlike v. 19, it is not clear whose life is to be sustained. In Ruth 4:15 the idiom is used somewhat differently, referring to the newborn

14. Translation from Stephanie Dalley, *Myths from Mesopotamia* (Oxford: Oxford University Press, 1989), 26. Cf. W. G. Lambert and A. R. Millard, *Atra-ḫasīs: The Babylonian Story of the Flood* (Oxford: Oxford University Press, 1969), 113.

15. Ephʿal, 104.

child of Ruth and Boaz who will be a *mēšîb nepeš* to Naomi, a support for Naomi in her old age and a continuation of her family line. The sad irony of our verse is that by giving up their children now, the parents will have no one in the future to provide for them and are, in essence, destroying their families. This terrible choice of keeping one's children with one or giving them up in the hope that they would survive often had to be made during the Holocaust.

Jerusalem as a beggar takes on the attribute of her people; she, like them, must beg for sustenance. There is also a stream of interpretation that connects *zôlēlâ* with *zôlēl*, "glutton" (e.g., Ibn Ezra), that must be understood in an ironic sense—she is a glutton who cannot get enough food, because there is no food to be had.

[12–22] Jerusalem's voice has been heard at the end of vv. 9 and 11, calling on God to attend to her woe. Beginning in v. 12 until the end of the chapter, Jerusalem becomes the speaker, addressing not God but human onlookers, thereby allowing the audience to experience the destruction through her eyes. The invocation to the passersby, which comes to include the audience as well, enlists the participation of those who hear Jerusalem's words. This section first calls on military imagery (God is the cause of the defeat) and then returns to many of the ideas in the first part of the chapter, including suffering and mourning, the absence of comforters, and shame and guilt.

[12] Before, the onlookers mocked Jerusalem and she called upon God to pay heed to her condition. Now she pleads with passersby to take note of her pain, which she attributes to God's anger. Calling on passersby is a common motif in destruction scenes (e.g., Zeph 2:15).

[13–15] The ways that God has harmed Jerusalem are enumerated, using metaphors from the realm of human warfare and conquest: fire to burn the city, nets to entrap the fighters, the yoke of subjugation placed on the necks of the vanquished, and trampling the enemy warriors. God is the enemy and he has defeated the city. Compare *Enuma Elish* IV, 100–120, which depicts Marduk as the conqueror who shot arrows, flung down the carcass of Tiamat and stood on it, scattered the forces, smashed the weapons, cast a net, and trampled the enemy.

[13] The "net" does not refer to a hunting implement, but to a military implement used to hold back captured men, preventing their escape. Such nets are pictured in ancient battle scenes,[16] and are mentioned by other biblical writers, for example, Ezek 12:13 and 17:20: "I will spread my net over him, and he will be caught in my snare, and I will bring him to Babylon." (See also Ezek 19:8; Hos 7:12.)

[14] The yoke symbolizes subjugation to the conqueror. Usually made of wood, it is here made of the sins of Jerusalem, fashioned by God and wrapped

---

16. Pictures of enemies caught in a net can be seen in J. B. Pritchard, *The Ancient Near East in Pictures*, p. 94, #298 and p. 98, #307.

in a tangle clinging like a heavy vine to Jerusalem's neck. This verse credits God with the destruction, and holds Jerusalem guilty for it. Nevertheless, Jerusalem is portrayed as a victim.

[15] The military metaphor continues with the word *silâ*, which I translate "trample," and which is related to *sālal*, the word for making a siege ramp (the ramp of packed earth built by the enemy to scale the wall of the besieged city). Images of trampling and crushing dominate the verse. Judah, the winepress, is trodden until the juice of the grapes (= blood; see Deut 32:14) is extracted. The warriors and youths are the crushed grapes, whose blood runs out like wine. Isaiah 63:3 also contains the image of God treading his enemies like grapes in a winepress (and cf. Joel 4:13).

[16–22] Jerusalem admits her sin, her rebellion against God; and at the same time she turns to God for help and comfort, and for vengeance against the enemy. Many phrases in this section echo those in the first part of the chapter, but with developments or reversals. Zion's weeping in v. 2 is repeated from her own perspective in v. 16. The enemy who boasts in v. 9 prevails in v. 16. The enemies who were commanded not to enter the temple in v. 10 are commanded to destroy Jacob in v. 17.[17] In v. 10 the foe stretched out his hand to plunder the temple; in v. 17 Zion stretches out her hand to seek comfort (either from her allies or from God). The pain, the loss of population, and the inability to find comfort are all replayed, but at a higher emotional pitch.

[17] A third-person voice interrupts Jerusalem's speech, explaining her situation. The imagery of isolation culminates with the comparison of Jerusalem to a menstruating woman, *niddâ* (to be distinguished from *nîdâ* in v. 8). The idea is that Jerusalem has become impure and is rejected by the surrounding nations, who are now enemies. The usual explanation, however, that *niddâ* means filth, "filthy thing" (NRSV, NIV, NJPS), or worse, "menstrual rag" (O'Connor, *NIB*), misses the mark. The term has as its basic meaning a menstruating woman, and it continues the metaphor of Jerusalem as a woman. Moreover, *niddâ* is not synonymous with filth. Filth is not associated with menstruation (except in the minds of modern scholars), but impurity is.

The Bible speaks of *niddâ* in two contexts of purity (see Introduction). In the context of ritual purity, menstruation, like other male and female genital discharges, renders a person impure and thereby unable to come in contact with the *sancta* (Lev 15:19–24). It does not, however, mean that the woman is disgusting or that she must physically separate herself from others. The Bible does not separate a menstruant from her family or from society. She is ritually impure but not a social outcast.[18] It is true, though, that *niddâ* can be used metaphorically for the moral impurity that defiles the land. Ezekiel 36:17 says that when

17. Linafelt, *Surviving Lamentations*, 51.
18. See C. Fonrobert, *Menstrual Purity* (Stanford: Stanford University Press, 2000), 16–20.

Israel dwelled in their land, they defiled it with their ways, which were "like the impurity of a *niddâ*." Ezra 9:11 also uses *niddâ* in reference to the defilement of the land. So by calling Jerusalem a *niddâ*, our verse may be saying that she is defiled land and therefore enemies will rise up to deliver the punishment that God has ordered. This interpretation is possible but perhaps not the best.

*Niddâ* also occurs in the context of moral impurity. Having sex with a *niddâ* is listed among prohibited sexual relationships, like incest, and these offenses against moral purity cause the land to be defiled. Leviticus 18:19, "Do not approach a woman in her menstrual impurity," is what is behind our verse. Zion is seeking a comforter, but God made those around her—her allies who should comfort her—into enemies, *so that she has no comforter*. She had become like a *niddâ* among them, in that no one wanted to have relations with her. Judah's erstwhile "lovers" do not want to have "sexual" relations with her because she is in a state of "impurity." (Cf. Kimhi's interpretation of Ezek 36:17.)

Verse 17 echoes vv. 9–10, which also speak of Jerusalem's impurity and the absence of comforters. In v. 10 the enemy spreads out his hand in an act of violation, and here Jerusalem spreads out her hand beseeching comfort. God had commanded the enemy not to enter his sanctuary (v. 10), but here God commands that the neighbors become enemies.[19]

[18–20] Even as Jerusalem declares her guilt from her own mouth, she still seeks sympathy from others, in this case "the peoples," perhaps the same as the "passersby" (v. 12), or perhaps the nations of the world, who are hereby instructed about God's ways. After calling on the peoples to see her pain, she calls on God. Verses 18 and 19 can be seen as containing parallelism in that Jerusalem's rebellion (v. 18) can be understood as her calling to her lovers (v. 19), and the captivity of the maidens and youths (v. 18) has as its counterpart the starvation of the priests and the elders (v. 19). On "lovers," *mĕʾahăbay*, with the connotations of illicit sex and adultery see Jer 22:20–22; 30:14; Ezek 16:33, 36; 23:5, 9, 22.

[20] Verse 20 picks up the thread from vv. 16–17, picturing Jerusalem as a supplicant, this time with the physical symptoms of her extreme mental and emotional state. The bowels, or gut, are the seat of emotions. The heart, often the seat of thought, is also used to indicate emotions.[20] Provan (54) suggests that *nehpak libbî*, "my heart is turned over," refers to a change in Jerusalem's emotional state (since *nehpak* can also mean "to turn into something else"), but I think that the city-woman has been feeling these emotions all along. The turning over of the heart, like the churning of the bowels, conveys emotional upset as a physiological process.

The end of the verse continues the scene in vv. 18–19, where some inhabitants are taken out of the city, and others die during the siege. Some translations

---

19. Linafelt, *Surviving Lamentations*, 51.
20. See M. Smith, "The Heart and Innards."

(RSV, NRSV, REB) take the contrast of "outside . . . inside" to mean outside the house (in the city streets) and inside the house, but it is better understood as outside the city, where the enemy is stationed, and inside the city, where starvation and disease run rampant. As Ezek 7:15 sees it, "The sword outside and plague and famine inside; whoever is in the field will die from the sword, and whoever is in the city will be consumed by famine and plague" (cf. also Deut 32:25 and Jer 14:18). The Sumerian city-lament Lamentation over the Destruction of Sumer and Ur (*ANET*, 618, lines 403–4) says: "Ur—inside it is death, outside it is death. Inside it we die of famine, outside it we are killed by the weapons of the Elamites." This is, then, a common trope in the description of a siege and it conveys the notion that there is no escape from death anywhere. Moreover, the suffering inside the city, which is the focus of our lament, is equal to, if not worse than, death by the sword.

[21–22] The end of the chapter focuses on the enemies, the feeling of joy they have at Jerusalem's downfall and the revenge against them that Jerusalem hopes for. The Hebrew words for "distress" in v. 21 and "evildoing" in v. 22 are the same, *rāʿâ*, and the play on words that results enhances the connection between Jerusalem's present condition and what she hopes will be her enemies' condition. Her only comfort seems to be in the hope that her enemies will suffer what they deserve. Chapters 3 and 4 have a similar ending, and the topos of revenge is present in communal laments and in Mesopotamian lament literature as well. This topos should be understood as more than a wish for vengeance, made in anger or for psychological benefit. The call to destroy the enemy, like the call to rid the world of evil (e.g., Pss 1:6; 104:35), is really expressing the desire to reinstate the natural order of things, the perfect world in which there is no evil and no enemies, the world in which Israel is secure under God's protection. For God to do to Judah's enemies as they did to her is to restore the equilibrium, right the balance, and to show God's power and dominion over the entire world. But this small ray of hope fades, and the chapter ends with the feeling of despair that has been heard since its beginning.

In contrast to most translations, I have interpreted "There is no comforter for me" in v. 21 as direct discourse, embedded in the larger direct discourse of Jerusalem's speech.[21] These are the words that Jerusalem groaned, and they constitute her "distress" heard by the enemy. On hearing this, the enemy rejoices.

The use of the independent pronouns *ʾānî* ("*I* was groaning") and *ʾattâ* ("that *you* had caused it") emphasizes the agency of each verb, and sets up an opposition between Jerusalem and God. *Kî ʾattâ ʿāśîtā* is difficult. Most commentators interpret it as "for you caused it," indicating that the enemies are rejoicing

---

21. On this topic see Cynthia Miller, *The Representation of Speech in Biblical Narrative*, Harvard Semitic Monograph 55 (Atlanta: Scholars Press, 1996), 226–31.

because God harmed his own people ("they rejoiced that you had done it"). Alternatively, one can interpret *kî* as an asseverative-emphatic particle.[22] The phrase would then not be a subordinate clause but would stand independent of (or loosely coordinated with) what precedes it—"You have indeed done it."

The perfect tense of *hēbēʾtā*, literally, "you brought the day you proclaimed," is difficult, but there is a long exegetical tradition that takes the phrase as a wish for the future, that God will bring that day he has already set for the judgment against Israel's enemies, just as he had brought the time he had set for the judgment against Israel (v. 15). An alternative explanation connects *yôm qārāʾtā* with what precedes it. As NJPS renders: "For it is Your doing: You have brought on the day that you threatened." In either case, the verse conveys Jerusalem's blaming God for the fact that the enemy is rejoicing over her plight, and expresses the hope that God will do the same to the enemy. The enemy, after all, does not deserve God's beneficence; they were permitted their victory over Israel only because God used them as a vehicle to punish her.

But the punishment of the enemy is for the future. For now, Jerusalem continues to languish. It remains for Second Isaiah, the prophet of comfort, to bring the rhetoric of Lam 1 full circle, to envision Babylon the way our poet envisioned Jerusalem. Isaiah 47 makes Dear Virgin Babylon the mourner, sitting on the ground, shamed by her uncovered nakedness, no longer the Mistress of Kingdoms, now a widow, bereft of her children, and about to suffer the "evil" (*rāʿâ*) that she deserves.[23] Here is what Lam 1:21–22 hoped for: " . . . let them be like me. Let their evildoing come before you, and do to them what you did to me."

# Lamentations 2:1–22
# Anger

א
1    Alas, in his anger the LORD makes loathsome[a]
         Dear Zion.
    He hurled down from heaven to earth
         the splendor of Israel;
    and disregarded his footstool
         on the day of his anger.

---

22. See T. Muraoka, *Emphatic Words and Structures in Biblical Hebrew* (Jerusalem: Magnes and Hebrew University; Leiden: Brill, 1985), 158–64; Waltke and O'Connor, *Biblical Hebrew Syntax*, 665.

23. For a discussion of Isa 47 as part of the city lament tradition, see Dobbs-Allsopp, *Weep*, 109–13; and, more briefly, Greenstein, "Lament," 93.

ב
**2**   The LORD consumed mercilessly
    all of Jacob's countryside;[b]
  he destroyed in his wrath
    Dear Judah's strongholds;
  he brought down to the ground, profaned,
    the kingdom and its rulers.

ג
**3**   He chopped off in fierce anger
    every horn of Israel.
  He turned back his right hand
    in the face of the enemy.
  And he burned in Jacob like a flaming fire,
    consuming all around.

ד
**4**   He bent his bow like an enemy,
    he poised[c] his right hand like a foe.
  And he killed all the treasured ones.
    On Dear Zion's tent
  he poured out his wrath like a fire.

ה
**5**   The LORD became an enemy;[d]
    he consumed Israel,
  he consumed all her[e] citadels,
    he destroyed his strongholds.
  And he made in Dear Judah so much
    moaning and mourning.

ו
**6**   And he demolished his booth like a garden (hut),[f]
    he destroyed his tabernacle.[g]
  The Lord sent into oblivion[h] in Zion
    festival and Sabbath,
  and he spurned in his raging anger
    king and priest.

ז
**7**   The LORD scorned his own altar,
    disowned his sanctuary.

He handed over to the enemy
    the walls of her citadels.
They made noise in the house of the LORD
    as on a festival day.

ח
**8**   The LORD determined to destroy
    the wall of Dear Zion.
He stretched out a line,
    he did not hold back his hand from consuming it.
He caused rampart and wall to mourn,
    together forlorn.

ט
**9**   Her gates sunk into the ground,
    he wrecked and shattered her bars.
Her king and princes are among the nations.
    Instruction is no more,
her prophets, too, found
    no vision from the LORD.

י
**10**   They sat on the ground, moaning,
    the elders of Dear Zion,
they put dirt on their heads,
    put on sackcloth.
They lowered their heads to the ground,
    the maidens of Jerusalem.

כ
**11**   My eyes were worn out from tears,
    my stomach churned,
my liver-bile was spilled out
    over the breaking of my dear people,
when little children and babies collapsed
    in the city squares.

ל
**12**   To their mothers they were saying,
    "Where is grain and wine?"
As they collapsed as if wounded
    in the city squares,

as their lives slipped away
    in their mothers' bosoms.

מ
13    How can I affirm you,[i] what can I liken to you,
        Dear Jerusalem?[j]
    What can I compare to you so that I may console you,
        Dear Maiden Zion?
    For as vast as the sea is your devastation.
        Who can heal you?

נ
14    Your prophets prophesied for you
        false and empty visions.[k]
    They did not reveal your iniquity
        so as to restore your fortunes.[l]
    They showed you false oracles
        and deceptions.

ס
15    All who pass by the way
        clapped their hands at you.
    They whistled and wagged their heads
        at Dear Jerusalem.
    "Is this the city that they say is the perfection of beauty,
        the joy of all the earth?"

פ
16    They opened their mouths against you,
        all your enemies.
    They whistled and gnashed their teeth.
        They said, "We have consumed her.
    This is indeed the day we waited for.
        We have found it; we have seen it."

ע
17    The LORD did what he planned,
        he carried out his word,
    as he ordained long ago.
        He destroyed and showed no mercy.
    And he made the enemy rejoice over you,
        he raised the horn of your foes.

צ
**18** Their heart cried out to the LORD.
  Wall of Dear Zion,
let tears stream down like a torrent
  day and night.
Give yourself no rest,
  your eyes no respite.

ק
**19** Arise, cry aloud at night,
  at the beginning of every watch.
Pour out your heart like water
  before the presence of the LORD.
Raise your hands toward him
  for the lives of your little children,
collapsing from starvation
  on every street corner.

ר
**20** See, LORD, and look,
  to whom you have done this.[m]
Should women eat their own fruit,
  the little children they care for?
Should priests and prophets be killed
  in the LORD's sanctuary?

שׁ
**21** Lying on the ground in the streets
  are young and old.
My maidens and youths
  have fallen by the sword.
You have killed on your day of anger,
  you have slaughtered without mercy.

ת
**22** You invite as on a festival day
  my attackers[n] round about.
And on the day of the LORD's anger
  no one escapes or survives.
Those whom I cared for and reared
  my enemy has consumed.

a. The word *yāʿîb* is best understood as a verbal form of *tôʿēbâ*, "abomination." Cf. Ps 106:40: "And the anger of the LORD was aroused at his people, and he abhorred (*way tāʿēb*) his inheritance." Another interpretation takes the word from the root *ʿwb*, "to be cloudy, darkened."

b. Hebrew *nĕ᾽ôt*, plural construct of *nāweh*, means pastureland or dwelling place (H. Ringgren, "*nāweh*," *TDOT* 9:273–77).

c. Taking the subject of *niṣṣāb* (masc.) as God, not *yāmîn*, which is feminine. My translation follows NJPS.

d. The *kāp* before "enemy" is asseverative. Dobbs-Allsopp, who takes the *kāp* as the comparative particle, "like," suggests that it is not original, since it is lacking in the Syriac, but was added later to avoid calling God the enemy. But the other versions reflect the presence of the *kāp*, so if not original, it is very early. The Targum, taking the phrase literally, explains: "He stood to the right of Nebuchadnezzar and aided him, as though he himself were an enemy of the house of Israel."

e. The text reads "her citadels" and "his strongholds," although the referents are not clear. Perhaps, as Provan suggests, "her citadels" refers to the palaces in Jerusalem and "his strongholds" refers to fortifications throughout Judah.

f. Literally, "He has demolished his *sukkâ* ('hut' rather than *śukkâ*) like the garden." My rendering assumes the ellipsis of a second *sukkâ*: "He has demolished his *sukkâ* like a garden [*sukkâ*]". Alternatively, Albrektson, *Studies*, 95, has suggested reading *kĕ-[ba-]gan*, "as if [in] a garden." This suggestion has been widely adopted. The spelling *śukkâ* for *sukkâ* occurs only here.

g. The word *môʿēd* occurs twice in the verse, and some scholars are reluctant to assign two different meanings to it, so they prefer "he has destroyed his festival" (instead of "his tabernacle"). But I see no reason to adopt this rendering. In fact, the same word with two different meanings also occurs in 1:1 (*rabbātî*, "thronged" and "princess") and 2:20 (*ʿôlal*, verb, "to do," and noun, "little children").

h. The verb is *šikkaḥ* in the *piʿel*, "to cause to forget, ignore." God's demolishing of the temple causes the celebration of festivals and Sabbaths to lapse, since there is no locus for their celebration.

i. The verb *ʿûd* means "to attest, bear witness." The poet wishes to serve as a witness who testifies to the actuality of the destruction and to its enormity. Exegetes who find the word strange emend it to *᾽eʿĕrōk*, "with what can I equate you" (as in Isa 40:18).

j. The *hê* before *bat yĕrûšālayim* is a vocative marker. See Waltke and O'Connor, *Biblical Hebrew Syntax*, 247.

k. *tāpēl* means lacking substance or the essential ingredient. Ezekiel 13:10 and 22:28 use it in the sense of "whitewash," a meaning applicable here, too, where the prophets have whitewashed the truth (Hillers). See also Jer 23:13.

l. Restoring the fortunes, *šûb šĕbût*, means returning to the status quo ante, the way Judah was before it sinned. It cannot mean here a return from captivity.

m. Or, "To whom have you done this?"

n. The word *mĕgûray* is difficult, with several possible meanings: *gwr* I, "to live, sojourn" (hence "neighbor"); *gwr* II, "attack"; *gwr* III, "fear." All three possibilities have their advocates. I have opted for "attackers" (with Hillers).

## Commentary

The tone changes from shame and despair in chapter 1 to anger in chapter 2. God is angry with Israel, and, from the tone in which that anger is described, we sense that the poet is angry with God. There is also a shift in focus from the victim (Jerusalem) in chapter 1 to the perpetrator of the destruction (God) in chapter 2. God has shown contempt for his temple and his people, and has brought ruin to both. God is Judah's enemy. He deprived the country of its strength and fought against it; he destroyed the city's fortifications and brought an end to social, political, and religious life. In its place came starvation and death. The negative tone of the chapter is expressed through the frequent use of negative particles in vv. 1, 2, 17, 21, and 22, which are stronger in the Hebrew than in my translation. Hebrew has verbs preceded by *lōʾ*, "did *not* remember, did *not* pity," whereas my translation is somewhat less stark—"disregarded, without mercy."

Chapter 2 may be divided into three parts: vv. 1–10: the description of Jerusalem in the third person; vv. 11–19: the poet's first-person speech as he reacts to what he sees; vv. 20–22: Jerusalem's speech to God. Kaiser ("Poet as Female Impersonator," 176) makes a slightly different division: 1–12, a description of Jerusalem; 13–19, an address to Jerusalem; 20–22, a speech by Jerusalem. However it is subdivided, the effect, like the effect of the different voices in chapter 1, is progressively to intensify the emotional impact as the poem moves from objective observer to subjective sufferer.

**[2:1–10]** The language in vv. 1–10 projects a feeling of strength and power in two ways. First, it employs many verbs signifying strong and violent action: hurled down, consumed, chopped off, destroyed, demolished, wrecked. It is with this brute force that God has acted. Second, it describes in detail the fortifications of the city—its walls, citadels, strongholds, ramparts, and gates. These architectural features are physically strong and, more important in this poem, are high. They will all come crashing down, sinking into the earth. We are, as it were, witnessing in slow motion the physical demolition of the city. There is an unmistakable sense of movement in this chapter from heaven to earth (begun in v. 1 and continued in the subsequent images) and even to beneath the earth, culminating when the gates sink into the ground, and the people lower their heads to the ground. In fact, the city is intentionally and methodically being unbuilt: God stretched out a line not to construct something but to destroy it (v. 8). It is as if God is erasing Jerusalem from the map. Gone is the temple, the religious center of the country; gone is the seat of the government; and gone even are the physical structures of the city. The once beautiful city is a heap of ruins.

**[1–2]** This picture of destruction begins with God turning his own place of residence, the temple, into an abomination. Then the destruction spreads to the entire land of Judah. "To make loathsome" (*yāʾīb*) is a verbal form from the same word as "abomination" (*tôʿēbâ*), a term often applied in Deuteronomy (7:25–26; 13:15; 17:4) to foreign worship, from which Israel must distance itself as from a disgusting impurity. Compare Ezek 5:11: "Since you defiled my sanctuary with detestable things and abominations, I, too, will diminish (you)." In our verse, God himself, not the people, has done what is most offensive to him.

Another interpretation, possible but less compelling, takes the word from the root *ʿwb*, "to be cloudy, darkened." The sense would be that God has darkened Zion, put a cloud over it; God is hiding himself from his people. This motif occurs at various points throughout the book, especially 3:44, "You have screened yourself in that cloud of yours, so no prayer could pass through" (but a different word for "cloud" is used). Here, though, the emphasis is on God's anger and destructiveness, so the stronger, more provocative "make loathsome" seems a better interpretation. Additionally, it parallels the profaning, or desecrating, of the kingdom in v. 2 and matches the thought in vv. 6 and 7.

"The splendor of Israel" refers to the temple. The temple in ancient Near Eastern religious thought was perceived as a link between heaven and earth, and this verse implies that God has broken that link. By destroying the temple, he has cut off Israel's access to himself.

The image of the temple as footstool is drawn from royal imagery of the ancient Near East, where the king sits on a throne with his feet resting on a low stool. God, often envisioned as a king, dwells in heaven with the earth as his footstool. The temple is, as it were, the place where God's feet touch the earth. As Ps 132:7 says: "Let us come to his tabernacle; let us bow at his footstool." Or, alternatively, God is envisioned as sitting in his temple, on a high throne, with his feet resting on the ark of the covenant (cf. Isa 60:13; Ezek 43:7; 1 Chr 28:2). In our verse God has disregarded, or better, discarded, his footstool. Our verse is echoed in Isa 66:1: "The heavens are my seat and the earth is my footstool, where could you build a house for me?" Isaiah suggests that God's "seat" and "footstool" still exist, even though the temple does not.

The scope of the destruction broadens in v. 2 from Jerusalem to all of Judah. Pham (*Mourning,* 102) insightfully observes that the picture of destruction moves from the countryside *(nāʾôt)* to the "strongholds," that is, the fortified towns of Judah, and then to the capital, Jerusalem. By being "profaned," the land, once God's holy dominion (cf. Ps 114:2), is no longer reserved for God but is now free for the taking by all the enemies.

[3–5] These following verses provide a vivid picture of how God, through a series of vicious actions, removed Judah's strength. God prevented Judah from defending herself and God would not defend her. Indeed, not only did God weaken Judah, he attacked her himself.

The horn, an image borrowed from the animal kingdom, is the symbol of strength and of glory (see, e.g., Jer 48:25; Ps 75:11; 1 Sam 2:1; Ps 112:9); it is used in referrence to Davidic kingship in Pss 89:25 and 132:17. Since "the kingdom and its rulers" were mentioned at the end of v. 2, it is possible that the "horn" in v. 3 alludes to the end of kingship in Judah. "His right hand" most likely refers to the hand of God rather than the hand of Judah (see Ps 74:11). The right hand is the hand that holds the weapon; God has refused to wield the weapon to defend Judah. More generally, God protects Israel with his right hand (Exod 15:6), and withdrawing it means that he refuses to protect Israel. Isaiah 41:10 envisions a time when once again God will protect with his right hand.

In v. 4 God is portrayed as a human enemy on the battlefield. He is an archer, as he is in Lam 3:12–13. As Ezek 39:3 shows, the bow was held in the left hand and the arrows in the right. The sequence presented here is that God strung his bow, aimed his arrows, and shot; as Pham (*Mourning*, 123) puts it: "ready, aim, fire!" The objects of his violence are the "treasured ones" (see 1:11). The expression is literally "those pleasing to the eye," and NRSV renders, "all in whom we took pride." I have retained "treasured" in order to preserve the connection with other occurrences of the word (1:7, 10; 2:4).

There is not a consensus on how to divide the last part of the verse. Some link "on Dear Zion's tent" with what precedes ("And killed all the precious ones in Dear Zion's tent") and some with what follows ("On Dear Zion's tent he poured out his wrath like fire"). I follow the accents in the MT, where the major pause is before "on Dear Zion's tent." The phrase "Dear Zion's tent" refers to the homes of the people of Judah, although it may be that it also conveys the idea of a military encampment. "Tent" is used in solemn expressions to mean "hearth and home" (K. Koch, "*ōhel*," *TDOT* 1:120). Job 19:11–12 expresses a similar sentiment to ours, also in military terms: "He kindles his anger against me; he regards me as one of his foes. His troops advance together, they build their road toward me, and encamp around my tent."

The picture of military attack in vv. 3 and 4 culminates in v. 5 with the utter destruction of Jerusalem and the fortresses of Judah, leading to "moaning and mourning" (*taᶜănîyâ waʾănîyâ*; see also Isa 29:2), an onomatopoeic representation of the sound of mourning and wailing, or keening.

**[6–10]** This section focuses on the religious and political impact of God's actions, although it continues to invoke images of the physical destruction of the architectural structures of the city. In fact, the physical destruction is rather graphic in v. 9, where the gates collapse from the weight of the falling walls, and their foundations sink lower into the ground (Pham, *Mourning*, 127).

**[6]** A *sukkâ* is a frail temporary hut in a garden or field used for shelter (cf. Isa 1:8; Jonah 4:5; Job 27:18); as a metaphor for protection, it is an appellation for the temple (Pss 27:5; 76:3). Verse 6 plays on both associations in this elliptical phrase: the temple, the place of protection, is here demolished as easily as one could demolish a garden hut. A similar idea is found in the Sumerian "Lamentation over the Destruction of Ur" (*ANET*, 457, lines 123ff.): "My house, founded by the righteous, like a garden hut, verily on its side has caved in . . . like a tent, the house where crops have been. . . ."[1]

The phrase *wayyaḥmōs kaggan śukkô* has puzzled many exegetes, who have proposed numerous interpretations. Some read it as: "He has demolished his *sukkā* like a garden"—that is, he turned his temple into a garden, a place of no habitation. "Garden" seems a bit too positive an image for destruction, but Micah uses similar images when he warns that Samaria will be turned into ground for planting vineyards (Mic 1:6) and Zion will be a plowed field (Mic 3:12). Alternatively, God plucks up his temple as one would pluck a vegetable in a garden (Rashi). The word *gan*, "garden," has been read by the LXX as *gepen*, "vine," yielding "he has spread out his tabernacle like a vine." This reading may simply indicate a confusion between words that look alike (*gn* and *gpn*), or it may suggest a different image, pruning away dead branches.[2] Pham (*Mourning,* 125) takes "garden" as referring to the pastures of Jacob, the land of Judah outside Jerusalem (v. 2).

The phrase may also be interpreted as a cosmic reference rather than, or in addition to, an agricultural image—if "the garden" is an elliptical reference to "the garden of the LORD." The garden of the LORD (or the garden of God) is Eden, the center of the world and the place where God resides. Eden is a mythic place that has its concrete realization in the temple.[3] The nexus between Eden and the temple is most clearly seen in Isa 51:3: "He made her wilderness like Eden, and her Arabah like a garden of the LORD. Joy and happiness will be found therein, thanksgiving and the sound of music." Isaiah is saying that the wilderness of Judah will become lush like Eden, and that in this Eden the temple worship (joy, thanksgiving, etc.) will resume. Another verse relevant to ours is Gen 13:10, where two words in our verse, *šḥt* ("to destroy") and *gan* ("garden"), both appear in reference to Sodom: "Before the LORD had destroyed Sodom and Gomorrah, (which were) like the garden of the LORD." Reading v. 6 in light of the Isaiah and Genesis verses raises the possibility that one may infer from v. 6 that God destroyed his once lovely temple (=Eden) as he destroyed the once gardenlike (or Edenlike) Sodom. The implication is that the destructive force used against the temple is like the force used against Sodom, and that the loss of the temple is the loss of the mythical center of the cosmos (Eden) that the temple represents.

[7] Worship in the temple was normally accompanied by music (Ps 150:3–6), recitations of praise (Ps 27:7), and the sound of the movement of crowds of people. These sounds, now absent, are, as it were, replaced by the

---

1. Cf. Dobbs-Allsopp, *Weep,* 69–70, and the references he cites.

2. See Provan, 64–65; idem, "Feasts, Booths and Gardens."

3. On the idea that the garden of Eden is fused with the temple see M. Greenberg, *Ezekiel 21–37,* AB 22A (New York: Doubleday, 1997), 591.

noise of the enemy clamoring over the walls and into the temple, noise that the poet ironically equates with the tumult of a festival day.

[8–9] Walls, ramparts, and gates protect the city, and also symbolize the city (cf. Ps 48:13–14 and also the Epic of Gilgamesh I, i 15–20). The gates are also the place of commercial, legal, and social activity. To destroy the walls and gates, as is described in vv. 8–9, is to destroy the life of the city in both a physical and social sense. The social disruption includes the absence of political leadership and the failure of the priests and prophets to engage in their profession of teaching Torah and obtaining divine revelations. God's word is distant from those who formerly served as vehicles for it. The physical vacuum brings with it a religious vacuum. Ezekiel 7:26 envisions a similar picture.

Ordinarily, the builder stretches out a line to build a straight wall, but here God stretches out a line to destroy the wall. The expression implies intentional planning on God's part, which makes his action seem more cruel. The rampart and the wall, here personified as mourners of their own destruction, stand together forlorn. "Rampart and wall" refer to the city's inner and outer wall (Philip J. King and Lawrence E. Stager, *Life in Biblical Israel* [Louisville: Westminster John Knox Press, 2002], 231.). The word *yaḥdāw* ("together") means both together and alone, that is, without anyone else besides the two (see 1 Kgs 3:18; Amos 3:3). Dobbs-Allsopp (*Weep*, 89) notes that in the Mesopotamian lament tradition, the city gate and the surrounding walls were likely the site of lamentation. He sees in v. 8 the image of someone sitting some distance away, hearing laments emanating from the city walls but unable to see the lamenters; to such a person it would seem as though the walls themselves are mourning. This realistic background is not necessary to explain a personification, and indeed the personification may be more effective if it is not based on reality. Jeremiah 14:2 and Isa 3:26 have similar personifications of gates in mourning. The city and its gates is a metonym for the people; both mourn the destruction. Verse 10 moves to the people's mourning.

[10] The mourning of the populace is total and is conveyed through a merismus—the extremes of the spectrum encapsulate everything between them: the "elders" and the "maidens" symbolize the old and the young, the men and the women, the mature and the inexperienced. But the emphasis is not only on who mourns, but how they mourn, the actions and motions that are performed. The physical gestures enumerated here—sitting on the ground, putting dirt on the head, wearing sackcloth—are typical signs of mourning. Mourning is expressed in the Bible not as a psychological or emotional state, but rather as a set of stylized behaviors (Anderson, *Time to Mourn*, 19–57). In addition, the lowering of the head, not a formal gesture of mourning, indicates a feeling of sadness or depression and also makes the motion of the mourners mimic the downward motion of the walls and gates, which have sunk into the ground. The word "moaning" is the sound of mourning or keening, from *dmm* II (not *dmm*

I, "to be silent, still"). Compare Akkadian *damāmu*, the sound that doves or cats make, and see Isa 23:1–2 in which *dmm* is parallel to *hll*, "to howl."[4]

[11–19] The anger of the first part of the chapter fades into mourning in the second part. Verse 10, which portrays the mourning of the people, serves as a transition to the poet's personal grief. The expression of his grief presents an opportunity to describe the misery of the siege and its aftermath (vv. 11–14), and then the shame that the reaction of onlookers engenders (vv. 15–16). The poet speaks directly to Jerusalem, trying, it would seem, to comfort both the city and himself. The fact that the destruction is the result of false prophecies that prevented repentance (v. 14) and that God carried out what he said he would (v. 17)—that is, the conventional explanation of the events—does not assuage the poet. Verses 18–19 bid Zion's wall to cry out to God.

[11–12] The poet speaks in the first person in an outpouring of emotion, expressed in physiological terms that signify anxiety and agitation. The stomach (or bowels) and the liver are the seat of the emotions. It may seem strange to pair the eyes with internal organs, but what they have in common here is that they secrete fluids: tearing eyes, a churning stomach, and a bilious liver. See Job 16:13 for the pouring out of bile on the ground.

The most heart-wrenching aspect of the destruction is the cruel death of the children, which here occurs in public, in the city squares, and not privately at home, out of sight. Perhaps we are to imagine the contrast with better times when the children played happily in the public square, with their mothers looking on protectively. Here, as elsewhere in the book, the children are starving and cry out for food, but their mothers cannot provide it. They ask for grain and wine. To some commentators it seems strange for children to ask for wine, but most commentators pass over the verse without note. What does it mean? At first blush, grain and wine would seem to represent the signs of God's blessing, or signs of joy and prosperity: "Where is the good and plentiful food we used to have?" But the usual expression is *dāgān* and *tîrôš* ("grain and juice of grapes," the raw materials for food), not as here *dāgān* and *yayin*. *Yayin* is more commonly paired with *leḥem*, representing drink and food (bread)—the finished products. The combination of *dāgān* and *yayin* is peculiar to our verse. The translation "bread and wine" found so often (NJPS, NIV, NRSV) misses the point. Renkema (273) notes the unusualness of the combination and attributes it to babytalk, but I find this suggestion unconvincing. What *dāgān* and *yayin* have in common, as opposed to *tîrôš* and *leḥem*, is that both grain and wine can be stored for long periods, while bread and juice spoil quickly. I interpret the children's request as meaning "Are there any remnants of stored-up food?" The phrase points to the fact that the city has no provisions left. On wine as a drink for famished people see 2 Sam 16:2.

4. See T. F. McDaniel, "Philological Studies, I," 38–40; and B. Levine, "Silence, Sound, and the Phenomenology of Mourning in Biblical Israel."

The phrase "their lives slipped away," *bĕhištappēk napšām*, is difficult. Provan questions whether it means "to expire," or simply "to experience extreme distress," as in Job 30:16. (The expression occurs elsewhere but only here in the *hitpaʿel*.) A long tradition interprets the phrase as indicating death. The Targum paraphrases the line: "as they scream like sword-wounded from thirst, in the cities' squares, as their lives expire from hunger into their mother's bosoms" (Levine, *Aramaic Version,* 67). I see a progression here, from collapsing like the wounded to dying. "Wounded," *ḥll*, means mortally wounded, those who first collapse and then expire. Once again the parallelism of *sword* and *famine* is invoked, but without using those words. Provan rightly calls to our attention that the emphasis here is on the process leading to death, not the fact of death in and of itself. The picture is made more moving by having the children expire in (or faint into) the bosom or lap of their mothers—the primary site of the babies' nourishment and protection (cf. Num 11:12).

[13] The poet searches for a way to serve as a witness, to verify the extent of the destruction, to reify it, to capture it in words—and through his verbal expression to bring comfort to Jerusalem. But the catastrophe is so enormous that there is neither a historical precedent nor a phenomenon in nature against which to measure it. Nothing like it has ever happened. Its scope is unimaginable. The only image that the poet can conjure up to convey it is the vastness of the sea, which is to say that it is infinite. More than that, the "sea" evokes the idea of the cosmic sea, and with it the notion of chaos and the antithesis of creation. The word for devastation, *šeber*, seems to be a play on words with *mišbār*, "wave." This wordplay enlarges the resonance of the sea image to suggest a devastation not only as vast as the sea, but also as destructive. The destruction of Jerusalem is, in a metaphoric sense, like the flood that returned the world to its primordial chaos (cf. Isa 54:9).

The poet, then, cannot console Jerusalem, and, in fact, the verses that follow only prolong the description of sin and suffering. Lamentations is not a book of consolation; it is a book that refuses to console, keeping the moment of grief always in focus.

[14–16] The question posed at the end of v. 13 is a rhetorical one. The potential healers are rejected one by one in vv. 14–16: the prophets have already failed in their mission and have prophesied falsely; the passersby, neutral observers, will only express amazement or mockery (see below); and the enemy will gloat at its accomplishment (see Dobbs-Allsopp, *Lamentations*). The reaction of the passerby to a destruction is a common motif (Jer 18:13–17 and elsewhere). It provides an external observer, another perspective, that confirms the poet's perspective. It also shows Judah's condition to be public, thereby underlining the theme of shame that accompanies destruction. In this case, the Judean belief in the inviolability of Jerusalem has been projected onto the passersby (cf. Lam 4:12).

Several nonverbal gestures are mentioned, conveying the reaction graphically. These gestures are then reinforced by words. Clapping the hands signifies derision or amazement (cf. Jer 19:8; 50:13; Zeph 2:15; Isa 37:22).[5] The word for "whistling," *šrq*, that occurs here and in the following verse signifies astonishment and sometimes derision.[6] It often occurs along with the root *šmm*, "be devastated" or another term (e.g., 1 Kgs 9:8; Jer 19:8; and note the contexts of destruction and cursedness in Jer 25:9, 18; 29:18).

It is hard to decide whether the reaction of the passersby is one of amazement or derision, because both their gestures and their words are ambivalent. Their words, or words like them, are applied in Psalms in a positive sense to Jerusalem—"joy of all the earth" in Ps 48:3 and *miklal-yōpî*, "perfect beauty," in Ps 50:2. The phrase *kĕlîlat yōpî*, "perfection of beauty," is used derisively in reference to Tyre in Ezek 27:3, 4, 11. Provan makes the case that the reaction of both the passersby and the enemy is one of hostility, and that the passersby are as pleased as the enemy to witness the fall of Jerusalem. This interpretation is possible, but not required.

There is no doubt about the reaction of the enemy, whose gestures and words are not the least ambivalent. Verse 16 ascribes to the enemy several offensive mouth gestures and noises. "Opening the mouth" is not a prelude to speech, but is another gesture of scorn or insult, like sticking out the tongue. Compare Ps 22:14, which suggests that this gesture is modeled on animal behavior.

[17] The enemy takes delight in what it thinks it has accomplished, but the poet understands that all this is God's doing, and that he had planned it long ago. The enemy's joy is part of God's doing. Just as God chopped off the horn of Israel in v. 3, here he raises the horn of the enemy.

[18–19] The poet addresses the wall and bids it pray to God. The first verb in v. 18 is problematic since it is masculine singular, while those that follow are feminine singular, referring to the wall. For that reason, the verb *ṣā‘aq*, literally "he cried out," is often emended to *ṣā‘ăqî*, "Cry out" (feminine imperative), referring to the wall. *Libbām* would be an adverbial, "from the heart." This emendation makes good sense but I have retained the MT's "Their heart cried out," which most likely refers to the collective people of Jerusalem (or, as the Targum says, Israel). This reading makes sense of the words, but the meaning in this context is unclear and the first line of the verse hangs by itself, unattached to the address to the wall that follows.

The address to the wall has puzzled many commentators. Hillers suggests emending *ḥômâ*, "wall," to <ni>*ḥḥemet*, "repentant," which is graphically similar. He thereby creates an epithet, "the repentant of Dear Zion," on the pattern

---

5. N. Fox, "Clapping Hands," 54.

6. M. Greenberg (private communication) confirms that the correct translation is "whistle," not "hiss" as some translations render it.

of *yōšebet bat X*, "the resident of Dear X." Those who retain the reading "wall" interpret it in one of several ways: as the actual city wall, a part for the whole; as the people of Judah (Moskowitz, who connects it with the allegorical interpretation of Song 8:10); or as a reference to God (Renkema and Pham, *Mourning*, 141; cf. Zech 2:9). These readings seem to me overly prosaic, when what we have here is the poetic personification of the wall, as at the end of v. 8. The wall that was earlier destroyed is now bidden to cry out to God.[7] The motif of cities or their structures lamenting is common in the Sumerian lamentations, for example, the Lamentation over the Destruction of Ur (*ANET,* 456), lines 48ff.: "O Thou brickwork of Ur, a bitter lament set up as thy lament." Since it was the city's fortifications that were mentioned in the first part of the chapter, it is fitting that they lament here. It is especially touching that the wall, the protector of the city that has not been able to provide protection, must now cry for help. The mention of night watches is particularly appropriate for the wall, the site of the watchmen. "At the beginning of every watch" means all night long. Isaiah 62:6–7 reverses the image by envisioning watchmen on the wall at the time of the restoration.[8]

The downward motion of v. 10 and earlier verses, which resumes in v. 21, is momentarily arrested in v. 19, where the upward motions of prayer are urged— "arise . . . raise your hands." Yet the picture of death has not changed; children are still starving in the streets, as they were in vv. 11–12, "in the city squares." The location here is "every street corner," which is used in connection with children also in 4:1 and Nah 3:10.

[20–22] The poem concludes with Jerusalem's prayer of supplication to God, the prayer the poet is instructing her to say. Its words are presumably calculated to arouse God's sympathy by calling his attention to the misery and destruction of the people, and the best way to accomplish this, at least from a human perspective, is through the mention of the starving children. Indeed, this is the main reason for the prayer, according to v. 19, and it is the first point mentioned in the prayer in v. 20. It was the last element, the climax of the description, in the first part of the chapter (vv. 11–12).

The picture of women devouring their children is a particularly gruesome form of cannibalism signifying extreme famine; it is a reversal of the natural order in which women feed their children. The motif of cannibalism, which recurs in 4:10, is found in descriptions of famine in the Bible (Lev 26:29; Deut 28:53–57; 2 Kgs 6:26–30; Jer 19:9; Ezek 5:10) and in Assyrian sources. In Esarhaddon's Succession Treaty, lines 549–50, we read: "in your hunger eat the flesh of your sons! In want and famine may one man eat the flesh of another"; line 547: "may they make

---

7. See also B. Kaiser, "Poet as 'Female Impersonator,'" 178.
8. See Sommer, *Prophet,* 127–30, for a discussion of Second Isaiah's allusion to vv. 17–19, and his reversal of the images in Isa 62:6–7; 51:17–22.

you eat in your hunger the flesh of your brothers, your sons and your daughters."[9]
In Ashurbanipal's annals we find: "The remainders who succeeded to enter Babylon ate (there) each other's flesh in their ravenous hunger" (*ANET*, 298); "Famine
broke out among them and they ate the flesh of their children against their hunger"
(*ANET*, 300). This motif may be an exaggeration that does not correspond to reality, but the image that it conjures up is extremely effective.[10]

Verse 21 plays on the idea of cannibalism in a manner that goes beyond the
conventional. The root *ṭbḥ*, "slaughter," is used of butchering meat in preparation for a meal (e.g., 1 Sam 25:11), but here it is not meat that is slaughtered,
but people, who are "sacrificed" on the festival day (v. 22).[11] The connection
with the trope of cannibalism is made more secure by the wordplay between *ṭbḥ*
and *ṭippuḥîm*, "those cared for" (v. 20). God who slaughters his people is no
less a cannibal than the mothers who eat their children.

The rest of the prayer recapitulates, with nuanced variations, other ideas
found earlier in the chapter. (1) The surrounding peoples (enemies or attackers)
coming as if on a festival day: in v. 7 they make noise in the temple like the
noise of a festival day; in vv. 21–22 they are invited as if on a festival day at
which the "sacrifice" was the slaughtered people of Jerusalem (see also 1:15
and cf. Zeph 1:7–8 and Isa 34).[12] (2) No more priestly instruction or prophetic
visions: in v. 9 the reason is that the location where they perform their duties
has been destroyed; in v. 20 the priests and prophets themselves have been slain,
ironically in the very sanctuary where they serve.[13] (3) Old and young sitting
or lying on the ground; in v. 10 they are mourning and in v. 21 they lie dead or
dying. (4) The angry Deity killing without pity, to the delight of the enemy: in
v. 17 God methodically and mercilessly destroys Judah and lets the enemy
rejoice over the destruction; in vv. 21–22 God invites the attackers to witness
the destruction and participate in it.

9. S. Parpola and K. Watanabe, *Neo-Assyrian Treaties and Loyalty Oaths*, 46, 52.

10. Eph'al, *Siege*, 61 n. 69, thinks it does not correspond to reality. P. A. Sorkin notes that cannibalism is documented in famines but involves less than 1 percent of the population (*Man and
Society in Calamity* [New York: Greenwood, 1968], 66–81).

11. See B. Kaiser, "Poet as Female Impersonator," 181–82. I have extended her observation to
make the link with cannibalism.

12. Drawing on Isa 34, Hillers notes (108), "the day of God's wrath is a grisly banquet at which
men are slaughtered like animals of sacrifice." Zephaniah 1:7–8 also has God prepare a sacrificial
meal and invite guests to the sacrifice of Israel.

13. To explain "priest and prophet" in v. 20 as one historical person, traditional interpretation
has invoked 2 Chr 24:20–22, which tells of the killing of Zechariah son of Jehoiada *the priest* who
was given the role of *a prophet* (Targum, Rashi). Y. Zakovitch suggests that the Chronicler used
Lam 2:20 to create a story about the sin of Joash, in order to justify the king's death. The Chronicler is thereby, in the view of Zakovitch, reinterpreting Lam 2:20. See Y. Zakovitch, "Poetry Creates History," in *"A Wise and Discerning Mind": Essays in Honor of Burke O. Long*, ed. S. Olyan
and R. Culley (Providence: Brown Judaic Studies, 2000), 318–19.

While the prayer may seem intended to appeal to God's mercy, it nevertheless retains the accusatory tone of the rest of the chapter.[14] It dares God to look at what he has done and to whom he has done it, as if to reprimand him: "Take a good look and consider the consequences of your action." The chiding tone continues in "to whom you have done this," emphasizing that it is Israel, God's special people, that he has hurt so badly. Unlike most communal laments, it never praises God or calls on his strength or goodness to save the people; in fact, it does not ask anything from God. It is not, then, a real prayer, but rather a rhetorical device through which the poet again expresses his anger, this time using the mouth of Jerusalem as his vehicle. To the extent that the description in the prayer concentrates more on the death of the people than on the destruction of the architecture, as the comparison with earlier parts of the chapter shows, we may say that the poet is even angrier at the end of his discourse than at the beginning.

In its final verses the chapter returns to the theme of God's anger with which it began. Verses 21–22 mention "the day of God's wrath," that is, the time of punishment (see also 1:12; 2:1), a concept akin to "the day of the LORD," a time in the future predicted by the prophets when God would punish those who deserved it (see M. Saebø, "*yôm*," *TDOT* 6:29). Now that time has come, and the punishment has been total. The last words express hopelessness—none have survived, all are consumed. Like chapter 1, this chapter ends with despair, but a despair born of anger rather than of sadness.

# Lamentations 3:1–66
# Exile

א
1    I am the man who has suffered agony
        by his rod of wrath.
2    Me he drove and forced to go
        in darkness with no light.
3    Against me alone he turns his hand again and again
        all the time.

ב
4    He has worn away my flesh and skin,
        he has broken my bones.

---

14. Also noted by Hillers (108), although he does not draw the same literary conclusion that I do.

5     He has set up against me and encircled me
          with bitterness and hardship.
6     In dark places he made me stay,
          like the eternally dead.


ב
7     He walled me in with no way out,
          weighed me down with chains.
8     Though I cry out and plead,
          he shuts out my prayer.
9     He has walled in my ways with hewn stones,
          he has twisted my paths.


ד
10    A lurking bear is he to me,
          a lion in hiding.
11    He forced me off my way[a] and tore me apart,[b]
          leaving me desolate.
12    He bent his bow and set me up
          as the target for his arrow.


ה
13    He shot into my innards
          the shafts of his quiver.
14    I have become the laughingstock of all my people,[c]
          the butt of their endless taunting.
15    He fed me my fill of bitterness,
          he sated me with wormwood.


ו
16    He ground my teeth on gravel,
          crushed me down into the dust.
17    My life was deprived[d] of well-being,
          I forgot goodness.
18    I thought: lost are my future[e]
          and my hope from the LORD.


ז
19    Remember[f] my misery and trouble[g]—
          wormwood and bitterness.
20    I well remember (them) myself,[h]
          and I am downcast;[i]

21    This do I tell myself,
         therefore I have hope:

ה
22    The LORD's acts of loyalty have not ended,[j]
         his compassion is not used up.
23    They are renewed every morning;
         vast is your faithfulness.
24    My portion is the LORD, I say to myself,
         therefore I hope in him.

ט
25    Good is the LORD to those who hope in him,
         to the one who seeks him.
26    It is good to wait and be still
         for the LORD's deliverance.
27    It is good for a man
         to bear the yoke in his youth.

י
28    He should sit alone and be still,
         for he laid it upon him.
29    He should put his mouth in the dust,
         perhaps there is hope.
30    He should offer his cheek to his smiter,
         eat his fill of shame.

כ
31    For the LORD will not spurn
         forever.
32    Rather, he hurts and (then) shows compassion
         as befits his vast loyalty.
33    For he does not willfully afflict
         or hurt human beings.

ל
34    The crushing underfoot of
         all the prisoners of the land,
35    the perverting of a man's justice
         before the presence of the Most High,
36    the subverting of a person in his lawsuit—
         does not the LORD see it?[k]

מ
37  Who is it who spoke and it came to pass[l]
        if[m] the LORD did not command it?
38  Is it not from the mouth of the Most High
        that come bad things and good?
39  How can a person still alive complain,
        a man about his punishments?

נ
40  Let us search into our ways and examine them,
        and return to the LORD.
41  Let us lift up our hearts and our hands
        to God in heaven.
42  We have sinned and rebelled;
        you have not forgiven.

ס
43  You have screened yourself off in anger and pursued us,
        you killed without pity.
44  You have screened yourself in that cloud of yours,
        so no prayer could pass through.
45  You have made us disgusting filth
        in the midst of the peoples.

פ
46  They opened their mouths against us,
        all our enemies.
47  Panic and pitfall were ours,
        calamity and collapse.
48  My eyes flow with streams of water
        over the collapse of my Dear People.

ע
49  My eyes will flow without cease,
        without respite,
50  until the LORD looks down from heaven
        and sees.
51  My eyes have brought me grief,[n]
        more than all the daughters of my city.

צ
52  . They hunted me like a bird,
        my enemies, for no cause.

53 They cast me alive into a cistern,
they placed the cover-stone upon me.
54 Water closed over my head,
I thought, "I am cut off."

ק
55 I called your name, LORD,
from the deepest cistern.
56 Hear my voice,[o]
don't shut your ear to my plea for relief.[p]
57 Come near when I call,
say "Do not fear."

ר
58 Champion my cause, LORD,
redeem my life.
59 See, LORD, the wrong done to me,
judge my case.
60 See all their vengefulness,
all their plots against me.

שׁ
61 Hear their taunts, LORD,
all their plots against me.
62 The mouthings and mutterings of my assailants
are against me all day long.
63 When they sit and when they rise, look,
I am their tune.

ת
64 Give them what they deserve, LORD,
as befits their actions.
65 Give them anguish of heart,[q]
your curse be upon them.
66 Pursue them with anger and destroy them
from under the LORD's heaven.

a. I have adopted the NJPS translation. The word *sôrēr* is usually taken as a *polel* form of *swr*, "to turn aside." A medieval view, adopted by Rashi and followed by a few modern exegetes, takes it from *sîr*, "thorn," which yields the idea that the thorns, not the wild animal, tore apart the speaker. Ibn Ezra rejects "thorn" in preference to *srr*, "stubborn" (he cites Hos 4:16); the LXX preceded Ibn Ezra in this interpretation, as did the Targum.

It is followed in NEB, albeit by a less than poetic translation ("He has made my way refractory"). Whether from *swr* or *srr*, the sense is that the speaker was diverted from his path.

b. The root *pšḥ* is otherwise unattested in the Bible, and its meaning "mangle, tear apart," is derived from the Aramaic, Syriac, and Arabic. The image of an attack by a wild animal continues. Early midrashim connected the word with *psḥ*, "to be lame." E. Levine (*Aramaic Version*, 130) notes that the attempt on the part of several modern scholars to connect it with Akkadian *pašāḫu*, "become still," is intriguing but this meaning is not reflected in any of the versions or early midrashim.

c. *ʿammî*, "my people," found in most Hebrew manuscripts and in the translations of LXX and Vulgate, is an old crux, because why would the poet's own people laugh at him? Many exegetes therefore read *ʿammîm*, "peoples," referring to other peoples (as in 1:7). This reading has a long history, as witnessed by the Masoretic note *sebirin* in some manuscripts, warning that while *ʿammîm* may make better sense, it is not to be substituted for *ʿammî* (Gordis, *Lamentations*, 177). Commenting on the Targum's paraphrase, "all who burst into my people," E. Levine (*Aramaic Version*, 131) notes that this rendering is equivocal and may refer either to Israelites or to foreign nations. All this suggests that the Masoretes (and also the LXX and Vulgate but not the Peshitta) had a textual tradition that read "my people" but that the sense of this reading was problematic. Hillers (127) retains "to all my people" and explains that "the cruel laughter of the man's own people is part of what he has to endure."

d. The verb *watiznaḥ*, in the *qal*, may be analyzed as a third-person feminine (literally "my life deprived") or second-person masculine ("you [God] deprived my life"). The latter analysis is rarely chosen because the passage speaks of God in the third person (although sudden shifts in grammatical person are not unheard-of in poetry). The former analysis is syntactically problematic and requires the revocalization of the verb to a third-person feminine passive, *nipʿal* (so *HALOT* 1:276, and most English translations).

e. For the sense of permanence associated with *niṣḥî* see G. W. Anderson, "*neṣaḥ*," *TDOT* 9:530–31. Other translations have "glory" (NRSV), or "strength" (NJPS), but they fall short of what the verse conveys. It is possible to see here a hendiadys: "hope for the future."

f. The verb *zākar* has been interpreted in two ways: as an imperative or as an infinitive construct. If it is an imperative, then the poet is now addressing God, asking him to remember, or pay heed to, the poet's suffering. If it is an infinitive, "remembering," then the poet himself is recalling his trouble. The Peshitta and Vulgate favor the first reading, while the Targum favors the second, as apparently does LXX's "I remembered." Modern commentators are divided. The wording is similar to 1:7, where Jerusalem remembers her misery and trouble.

g. For *mĕrûdî* see the comment at 1:7.

h. The verbs in v. 20 may be analyzed as second-person singular, also addressing God; or as third-person feminine, referring to *nepeš*. I have chosen the latter, following most commentators. The translation is literally "my soul surely remembers and is cast down within me."

i. The Qere *tāšôaḥ*, from the root *šḥḥ* or *šwḥ*, means "to bow low, be humble," and by extension, "feel despondent." The phrase echoes Ps 42:6–7, which contains three of the same terms found in our context: "the self being downcast," *nepeš šāhah*; "remember," *zākar*; and *yl* "hope." The *Kethib*, *tāšîah*, is from *šwh*, and has also been read as *śyh*, "to speak, complain." While "My soul complains" is probably not the primary meaning, it garners support as a secondary meaning, a double entendre, from what follows in vv. 22 and 24 where the poet seems to be arguing with himself, looking for the right answer to convince himself.

j. The verb *tamnû* means "we ended," and is reflected in some Greek and Latin versions, and in the KJV's "It is of the LORD's mercies that we are not consumed." Provan, attempting to smooth the awkwardness of the phrase thus construed, suggests that it be read in relation to what precedes it instead of what follows, and he translates: "But this I call to mind, and therefore have hope: the steadfast love of the LORD! For we are not consumed because his mercies never come to an end: they are new every morning." This translation sticks to the grammar but goes against the syntax, which is symmetrical: *kî lōʾ X, kî lōʾY*. An alternate tradition, reflected in the Targum, in Rashi and Ibn Ezra, and also in many modern translations (NRSV, NJPS, Hillers), renders the verb as "they ended" (referring to God's acts of faithfulness), which makes more sense and preserves the symmetrical structure. The *nûn* can be seen as a type of dissimilation for the double *m*: *tamnû* instead of *tammû* (Ibn Ezra).

k. I have made this a rhetorical question for greater effect. Most translations render it in the indicative: "The LORD does not approve."

l. The result of God's creative command is here *wattehî*, "she came to pass," whereas Ps 33:9 has *wayyĕhî*, "he came to pass."

m. I supply the word "if" to make the meaning more intelligible. The Hebrew is extremely paratactic, having no particle between "it came to pass" and "LORD."

n. The phrase is difficult. I have accepted the usual rendering although it is less than intelligible. A note in NJPS suggests emending *ʿênî*, "my eye," to *ʿonyî*, "my affliction," according to which vv. 50–51 would read: "Until the LORD looks down from heaven/ And beholds my affliction./ The LORD has brought me grief." Hillers adopts a similar reading.

o. I follow Hillers and others in taking the verbs as precative perfect. It is possible, though, to translate like NIV: "You heard my plea: 'Do not close your ears to my cry for relief.' You came near when I called you, and you said, 'Do not fear.'" NRSV is similar. Likewise, the verbs in vv. 57–61 are translated in the past tense.

p. *rĕwāhâ* is unusual in its usage here, at least as it is understood by most commentators, who take it as meaning "groan." Provan suggests "gasping," from the root *rwh*, "to breathe," following the Vulgate's *a singultu meo* ("Past, Present," 174). The word generally means "respite, relief, easing of a condition" (Exod 8:11); I preserve this meaning by understanding the phrase *lĕrawhātî lĕšawʿātî* as a hendiadys, "to my plea for relief."

q. So NJPS and NRSV. The meaning of *mĕginnat lēb* is uncertain. Some interpretations emphasize the notion of *gnn* = "cover," hence NIV: "Put a veil over their hearts." Provan summarizes a range of interpretations built on *gnn*, which he connects with *māgēn*, "shield" (as does Rashi's second interpretation and also Ibn Ezra). This "hard cover" suggests to Provan hardness of heart.

## Commentary

Chapter 3 stands apart from the other chapters in the book in several ways. It does not begin with "alas," as chapters 1, 2, and 4 do, and so is not formally marked as a lament. The speaker is not Jerusalem, or her people, or a poet observing Jerusalem and her people. Rather, the chapter gives voice to a lone male,[1] speaking in the first person, about what he has seen and felt and what sense he can make of it.

Because the first-person speaker announces himself so forcefully in his maleness (*geber*), many interpreters have puzzled over who this *geber*, this speaking voice in chapter 3, represents. Few nowadays identify him with a historical individual, like Jeremiah, Jehoiachin, or Zedekiah (but cf. M. Saebø, "Who Is 'the Man'?"). Some see him as the same poet who spoke in the earlier chapters (Provan), while others take him to be an anonymous sufferer, perhaps a surviving soldier (Lanahan and Owens), a defeated strongman (K. O'Connor, in NIB), a collective voice of the people (Albrektson, Gordis), a prominent resident of Jerusalem (Renkema), or Everyman (Hillers).[2] Dobbs-Allsopp (*Lamentations*) insightfully notes that the incipit "I am" is the conventional form of self-presentation in royal inscriptions. He also finds other signs of royal or Davidic genealogy in this chapter, but in the end opts for Hillers's Everyman as the identification of the *geber*. Dobbs-Allsopp's observation about royal inscriptions, however, is worth considering and expanding to include other "autobiographies" in the ancient Near East (like the Akkadian "Mother of Nabonidus" [*ANET*, 560–62] and Eccl 1:12).[3] It may be that the beginning of chapter 3 is imitating an accepted literary convention. If so, that convention has been turned on its head, for instead of self-glorification, we find self-abasement.

I see the speaker as the personified voice of the exile, and I would explain his literary persona in two ways. First, the male voice is a counterpart to the female voice of the city in chapter 1. Zion, personified as a woman, speaks in chapter 1, and here a male voice also speaking in the first person echoes, from a different perspective, the experience of destruction and exile. Just as the imagery in chapter 1 was feminine—the widow, the unfaithful wife, the raped woman—so here the imagery seems more masculine, invoking the physical violence against the male body associated with war and exile. Physical brutality is

---

1. Some exegetes see two different speaking voices in this chapter, because in v. 40 the first-person speaking voice changes from singular to plural, and in v. 43 there is a shift from speaking of God in the third person to addressing him in the second person. Shifts like this are common in biblical poetry and do not prevent taking the entire chapter as the discourse of one speaker.

2. Westermann, 68–73, surveys the views of German scholars, many of whom favor the idea of a communal spokesman.

3. See T. Longman III, *Fictional Akkadian Autobiography* (Winona Lake, Ind.: Eisenbrauns, 1991).

conveyed through strong verbs of action: being smitten (v. 3), being shot with arrows (vv. 12–13), being walled in (vv. 7, 9), chained (v. 7), and crushed (v. 16). Many parts of the body are mentioned, to make more graphic the physical abuse: flesh and bones (v. 4), innards torn apart (vv. 11, 13), being fed poison (v. 15), gravel on teeth (v. 16), mouth in the dust (v. 29), cheek smitten (v. 30), mouth of the enemy (v. 46), eyes (vv. 48, 49, 51), and head (v. 54). Taken together, chapters 1 and 3 give us gendered pictures of a female and male victim—the city, battered and ruined, that remained behind; and the people, entrapped and injured, who were conquered and deported.

Second, this male persona is a Job-like figure, crying out in his suffering to a God who refuses to respond, struggling to make sense of the awful tragedy that has befallen him, trying to maintain his faith in the face of God's cruelty, and seeking to justify God's actions. It is perhaps more than coincidental that Job, in his first speech (Job 3:3), also refers to himself as a *geber*. Like Job, our poet is hunted by wild animals (3:10; Job 10:16); he is the target of God's arrows (3:12; Job 16:12–13); he is sated with bitterness (3:15; Job 9:18); he is cut off from access to God (3:44; Job 3:23); and he is the butt of the enemies' taunts (3:63; Job 30:9). Like Job's friends, our poet reasons that there is hope for the wretched, that it is good to bear chastisement from God (3:24–27; Job 5:16–18), and that God may cause hurt but then he will bring healing (3:32; Job 5:18). He is sure that God would not pervert justice (3:33–36; Job 8:3). Like Job, our poet insists that both good and bad come from God (3:38; Job 2:10) and must therefore be accepted. This voice of the nation is, like Job, a literary fiction; but unlike Job, he is not perfect. His sins—the nation's sins—must figure in the theodicy. This is not a poem about the suffering of the righteous; it is a poem about the suffering of the guilty.

Another feature that distinguishes this chapter is the change in poetic form. A triple acrostic, with three short lines assigned to each letter of the alphabet, gives a more rapid and insistent beat to the poem. Each succinct statement strikes hard. The terseness of the lines is compensated for by their grouping in threes, and again by the way the thought from one group is carried over to the next group. This connection of thoughts is seen clearly in, for example, vv. 12–13, the last of the *dālet* lines and the first of the *hê* lines; v. 12 speaks of the bow, and v. 13 continues with the arrows. Again, in v. 48, the last of the *pê* lines, the image of eyes streaming with water, carries over into v. 49, the first ʿ*ayin* line. If one groups the verses according to their subject matter, one would group together vv. 39–41, 42–44, 45–47, and 48–51, a grouping at odds with the alphabetic structure. This "enjambment" of ideas and images across the alphabetical boundaries is a counterweight to the formal structuring of the acrostic. It keeps the poem moving forward and prevents the poem from breaking up into three-line sets. The poem thus keeps moving from one "stanza" to another and from one thought to another, in a manner that makes a neat subdivision of the chapter impossible. Moreover, the poem lacks a clear progression of ideas, preferring to alternate between despair and hope, as if the speaker wants to convey his changing feelings as he ponders the events and their implication. This chapter, more than all the others in the book, combines descriptions of suffering with theological inquiry into that suffering. But like the other chapters in Lamentations, this one, too, refuses to resolve the issue it sets before the reader.

[3:1–21] Although it is not immediately apparent, vv. 1–13 are constructed on the metaphor of a sheep and shepherd, a common biblical image (Albrektson, Hillers). A good shepherd, exemplified in Psalm 23, guides his sheep with his rod, leads the sheep to good pasture and water, helps them through narrow, dark, and twisting mountain paths, and protects them from wild animals. God, the shepherd of this chapter, is the antithesis of the good shepherd. He has a rod that harms, that forces the sheep into dark places. The sheep feels walled in, imprisoned, caught in a maze, unable to find a straight path. God himself is the bear and the lion endangering the sheep. Instead of shooting at the wild animals, God shoots at the sheep.[4] Isaiah 49:9–10 reverses the image, restoring to God his role as good shepherd who will bring the people out of darkness, lead them to open pastures, protect them from the heat of the wind and sun, and guide them to water.

Where is the bad shepherd leading his sheep? Into exile. These verses are best understood as a poetic representation of the forced march into exile. The speaker is driven on a path against his will, mistreated by the conquering soldiers, and battered by the physical hardship of the journey. He is led in chains along a difficult and tortuous path from which he dare not stray lest his captors kill him; he falls down, or is forced down, into the dust (v. 16). He is utterly broken, both physically and mentally. Exile was understood to be the punishment for rebellion, so it seems reasonable to assume that, since the poet feels God is punishing him, he is most likely referring to the punishment of exile. In fact, the curses of Deut 28, which inform Lamentations at various points, describe the exile in terms that have echoes in these verses. The phrase *rā'â 'onî*, "suffered agony" (v. 1), sounds like *mar'ēh 'ênêkā*, "the vision of your eyes" (Deut 28:34); *nāhag wayyōlēk*, "drove and forced to go" (v. 2) is reminiscent of "The LORD will force you to go" (*yōlēk*) and "to which the LORD will drive you" (*yěnahegkā*, Deut 28:36–37). The ideas of being blind and feeling around in the darkness (Deut 28:28) and suffering physical abuse and disease (Deut 28:33) are further indications that Lam 3 opens with a poetic picture of the exile. Another piece of evidence for the picture of exile is chains (v. 7), which were sometimes put on prisoners being deported, according to the Assyrian reliefs. Chains and bonds are associated with the Babylonian conquest, both literally

---

4. Hillers, 124, sees vv. 1–9 as a reversal of Ps 23; I would extend the reversal to v. 13. See also Barré and Kselman, "New Exodus," especially 99–100.

and figuratively (see Nah 1:13; 3:10, and elsewhere).[5] The term for bronze or copper chains used in v. 7 also appears in 2 Kgs 25:7 and Jer 39:7 in reference to Zedekiah and in 2 Chr 36:6 in reference to Jehoiachin.

Extrabiblical sources record deportations, although they do not present the perspective of the deportees. Bustenay Oded has gathered and analyzed the Neo-Assyrian sources—texts and reliefs—and the information he provides, which may be applied to the Babylonians as well, is especially relevant to our discussion.[6] The reliefs typically show the male captives with their hands, and sometimes their feet, bound in chains. Since these figures do not appear in all reliefs, Oded concludes that only high-ranking captives were bound. The captives are usually in family groups, the men always on foot and the women and children either in carts or on foot—in the latter case the young children are carried by their mothers.[7] Only small amounts of food and water could be brought by the captives, either because the supplies had been exhausted or because of the limitations on what they could carry. Some reliefs depict naked and barefoot prisoners, but Oded points out that it was in the interest of the Assyrian king that all captives arrive in good physical condition (since they were to be useful to the empire in several capacities), and that therefore steps were taken to ensure the successful transfer of the captives to Assyria and to prevent their abuse. Periodic reports, including lists of escapees and those who had fallen ill, were written to the king. Providing food on the journey was a problem, so the governors whose territories the captives traversed were obliged to provide them with food and other necessities. This care and concern for the prisoners did not arise from the humane feelings of the captors, but from the fact that prisoners were human booty belonging to the king of Assyria. The care notwithstanding, the journey was a difficult one, physically and psychologically, for the captives, even though from the Assyrian point of view they may have been treated properly.

Whether the captives were actually made to walk naked and barefoot, as pictured in some reliefs, is doubtful according to Oded. He explains these depictions as an artistic convention to represent the submission of the captives, not as realistic portraits of the treatment of the prisoners. Lamentations 3 may be a literary counterpart, where similar conventional descriptions are used to dramatize the misery of the exiles from their own point of view. That is to say, the picture that chapter 3 presents, if it is indeed meant to represent the process of going into exile, is a highly rhetorical piece of literature. The way in which "the Judean exile" expresses his hardships echoes the ways that the conquerors expressed them, but from the opposite perspective. The perspective is that of

5. D. Smith-Christopher, "Reassessing the Historical and Sociological Impact," 28–29.
6. *Mass Deportations*, 34–41.
7. For illustrations see D. Ussishkin, *The Conquest of Lachish by Sennacherib*, 84–88.

the victims, not the victors. The purpose here is to show not the power of the conqueror, but the misery of the conquered.

The physical reality is only one aspect of the presentation. The chapter is just as concerned with the theological view of exile (see Introduction, The Theology of Destruction and Exile). The point that looms largest is that it is God, not the Babylonians, who is responsible for the exile (just as in chapter 2 it was God, not the Babylonians, who caused the destruction). The perspective in which God is the enemy has an interesting effect on the convention of deportation scenes, in which the conqueror is portrayed as cruel and therefore strong. Lamentations 3 paints a deportation scene in words, but it is a scene without enemy soldiers. God is the enemy, not portrayable in visual art, but describable in poetry. The divine enemy is also the supreme power in the world and, despite the harm he has caused, he remains the only source of help for the poet.

But the poet is exiled not only from his land, but also from his God. If one continues the analogy to Assyrian and Babylonian deportations, it becomes evident that, whereas the deportees were brought before the king of Assyria or Babylonia in a formal audience in his throne room (according to the reliefs), the Judeans were not brought before the divine "king" against whom they had sinned. On the contrary, they were cut off from his "throne room," the temple, and denied access to him elsewhere because God refused to grant them an audience. The poet faces a situation without precedent: the inability to communicate with God. It is this unbridgeable distance between God and his people that the poet plumbs in much of the poem.

**[1–4]** The poem begins: "I am the man." The Hebrew *geber* registers forcefully the maleness of the speaker. Gender-neutral translations, like NRSV, diminish the impact by translating, "I am one."[8] Provan points out that it is usually God who "sees the affliction" of humans, but here it is a man who has "seen the affliction" (i.e., "suffered the agony") brought by God. The first-person nature of the discourse is stressed by the triple use of the first-person pronoun, at the head of each clause, once as subject, once as direct object, and once as indirect object. The effect is to personalize the suffering and make its telling more authoritative since the report comes from a person (a fictive persona) who has, figuratively, experienced it firsthand. Just as this man is nameless and lacks all identification, so the "he," the perpetrator of the suffering, is nameless until v. 18; before that verse, God is referred to only indirectly (although unmistakably), by a third-person pronoun.

The man's experience is conveyed through the verb *rāʾâ*, "to see." NJPS suggests a possible emendation to *rāʿâ*, "to shepherd," in the sense of "whom the LORD has shepherded with." While there is no reason to adopt this emendation, the suggestion shows that NJPS, too, perceives the shepherd metaphor. The shep-

---

8. So O'Connor in *NIB*.

herd's rod, normally an instrument of protection, is here synonymous with God's "rod of wrath," the instrument by which God manifests his anger. Compare Isa 10:5, where Assyria is God's rod of anger—that is, the instrument through which he will punish Israel. Here the rod is Babylonia. The image of the smiting rod is strengthened by the words "he turns his hand," *yahăpōk yādô*, which has the idea of hitting someone. Renkema, who sees in vv. 3–5 an image of war rather than of a shepherd, takes *yahăpōk yādô* as referring to a charioteer pulling the reins of the horse (cf. 1 Kgs 22:34; 2 Kgs 9:23) and imagines a prisoner being driven by his captor; but this interpretation has little to recommend it.[9] Reading against the acrostic, in accord with the "enjambment" described above, one may interpret v. 4 as an explanation of v. 3: God has beaten the poet so badly that his body is bruised and broken.

[5–17] These verses describe the poet's agony in more specific, yet still highly metaphoric, terms. In the course of these verses the shepherd image gradually recedes and the image of a captive of war becomes more prominent. Subtly but strikingly, captivity is likened to death (v. 6), which is a dark place from which there is no escape (v. 7) and from which God cannot hear supplicants (v. 8). The notion that the supplicant is near death, or like a dead person, is a common feature of psalms of lament. Psalm 88 provides an especially useful background for interpreting this section of Lamentations, for the two texts share not only the same general picture but also a number of the same phrases (Renkema, 359). Most obvious are "darkness" (Lam 3:2; Ps 88:7), "the soul/life being deprived" (Lam 3:17; Ps 88:15), "forgetting" (*nšh*, Lam 3:17; Ps 88:13), "the deepest cistern" (Lam 3:55; Ps 88:7). Death is pictured here and elsewhere (e.g., Ps 6:6) as a place of darkness, a place of ashes and dust, a pit or cistern, where the dead stay forever, cut off from the world and from God. The dead are forgotten (ignored) by God (Ps 88:6), which is perhaps why so many supplicants call on God to "remember."

This trope of death, and the lament that accompanies it, signify that the supplicant is distant from God. As Anderson (*Time to Mourn*, 92–93) puts it, the psalmist (in psalms of lament) is in a state of mourning, and as a mourner, he cannot appear before God and praise him (or join in the public rituals of praise). In this sense, the psalmist is exactly like the dead, who also cannot praise God (Ps 6:6). Anderson takes this trope as more than a poetic metaphor. He understands it as having "practical consequences" for the mourner's state of existence. That is to say, the psalmist is actually in a state of mourning, with all of the rules that apply to that state. Psalms of lament do not praise God; rather,

---

9. Earlier, A. Fitzgerald, "Hebrew *yd* = 'Love' and 'Beloved,'" *CBQ* 29 (1967): 368–69, noted that the combination of *hāpak* and *yād* occurs only in reference to a chariot, but seeing no chariot here he came up with the even less likely interpretation that *yd* means "love." Fitzgerald's interpretation was rightly rejected by Hillers already in 1972 (54).

they express the hope that the psalmist may praise God in the future. But in order for the psalmist to do so, God must save him from his present crisis so that he may cease to be a mourner. In Lamentations this concept takes on a whole new dimension, because now that the temple is destroyed, the supplicant, indeed the entire nation, are permanently cut off from God and hence will remain in a permanent state of mourning (in the sense that mourning is synonymous with being cut off from God). This is why our poet feels like one of the dead (v. 6).

I prefer to translate *mētê ʿôlām* (v. 6) as "eternally dead" rather than the more usual "long dead," for the idea is that the dead stay dead forever and will never see the light of day again. In this respect there is no difference between those long dead and those recently dead (see also Ps 143:3).

Understanding that the trope of death is at work in this chapter has implications for the interpretation of other verses in this section and in later ones. One example is v. 17, "My life was deprived of well-being (*šālôm*), I forgot goodness (*ṭôbâ*)." This means more than that the poet forgot how it felt to be happy. What he is deprived of is the goodness of being close to God, for he is in the land of forgetting, the land of oblivion (Ps 88:13), where instead of goodness he is sated with wormwood or evil as those in Sheol are (Ps 88:4; cf. Lam 3:15). This is another way of saying that he is like the dead. The same idea continues in v. 18, where the poet thinks that he has no hope for the future with the Lord. (The opposite idea, being in God's presence, is equated with goodness and life in Pss 23:6 and 27:13.) The death trope can also be seen in vv. 22–23, 28, 54 (see the comments on these verses), where it is intertwined with other metaphors. The power, beauty, and complexity of this chapter lie in the mixture of types of discourse and the combination of tropes and metaphors.

[5–9] The poet feels walled in, locked up in a dark place from which there is no escape—a graphic, physically concrete metaphor for captivity. Hewn stones (v. 9), or dressed stones, are smooth and fit more closely together than unhewn stones, so the wall is stronger and less likely to crumble. The road is blocked, constricted, and twisted. There is no way to find a straight path. The language of vv. 7–9 is reminiscent of Hos 2:8: "I will hedge her path with thorns, set up fences, and she will not find her way." Isaiah reverses this image in his prophecy of comfort (40:4), where the twisted road is made straight for the exiles' return. Is there perhaps some irony in the use of "hewn stones," which were forbidden for the altar (Exod 20:22) but used in Solomon's temple (1 Kgs 5:31; 6:36)?

Hebrew *rōʾš*, "poison," in v. 5 was read as the homophonous word meaning "head" by LXX. "Poison" seems inappropriate to some modern commentators, who prefer to read *rēʾš*, "poverty" (Hillers). But "bitterness, gall," an extended meaning of "poison," fits the context. Taking *rōʾš* and *tĕlāʾâ* as a hendiadys, the phrase might be construed as "toxic hardship." The word *tĕlāʾâ*, "hardship," is used in reference to the period of Egyptian slavery (Num 20:14) and to the domination of Assyria, Babylonia, and Persia (Neh 9:32). So this term may contain a strong hint of the exile, or the hardship on the road to exile (cf. Exod 18:8, where *tĕlā'â* is used for the hardship on the road out of Egypt).

[10–13] From the feeling of being enclosed or trapped in vv. 5–9, the poem moves to a different kind of being trapped—an animal trapped by a hunter. The shepherd, who is supposed to protect his flock from lions and bears (cf. 1 Sam 17:34–35 and Amos 5:19), is metamorphized into the wild animals that threaten the sheep. Then the shepherd/God becomes the hunter, and the poet becomes the prey. The images dissolve and re-form: God is the shepherd, God is the lion and bear; then the poet is the lion and bear and God is the hunter. Whether "sheep" or "lion," the poet is stalked by his natural enemy. When put this way, the images say that God is the poet's natural enemy.

[14–17] This section utilizes images of the mouth: people laugh at the speaker (v. 14), he is fed bitterness (v. 15), his teeth are ground on gravel (v. 16), and his life (*nepeš* also means "throat") has no well-being. Verse 15 is to be compared with Jer 9:14: "I make this people eat wormwood; I make them drink a bitter drink." In Jeremiah, "wormwood" and "bitter drink" refer to the exile, as they must in Lamentations, too. Lamentations goes further than Jeremiah; it is not just a matter of making someone eat, it is feeding him till he is full. Instead of providing the poet with plentiful nourishment, God has, as it were, force-fed him with the bitterness of exile till he can hold no more. Wormwood, a plant with a bitter taste, is often used metaphorically for bitterness or sorrow (cf. Amos 5:7; 6:12; Prov 5:4). This word and its synonyms occur frequently in this chapter (also in vv. 5, 19).

The feeding image is continued by the mention of the grinding of teeth in v. 16. Both verbs in this verse are rare, and therefore not fully understood, but their general sense seems clear. Provan questions whether the image is a continuation of the feeding in v. 15 or refers to subjugation and abasement ("rubbing someone's face in the dirt"). Indeed, putting one's face/mouth in the dust occurs in this sense in v. 29 and "licking the dust" is in Ps 72:9 and Mic 7:17. Cf. also Ps 7:6. There is, however, no reason to choose between these two images, as they are both at work here. All of the expressions about eating bitterness form an extended metaphor for the abased state of the poet. Compare Ps 102:10: "I have eaten ashes like bread and have mixed tears with my drink." One might see both a literal and a figurative dimension to the image in our case: the prisoner on his march into exile really does "eat dirt"—poor food under dirty conditions—and at the same time "eating dirt/wormwood" serves as a metaphor for subjugation and misery. The captor is God, who is causing the speaker to be in this condition.

[18–21] These verses form a transition from the description of suffering to the disquisition on the nature of God. They play on the ideas of forgetting and remembering and hoping—the language of lament, and on thinking and speaking—the language of wisdom. Speaking is especially characteristic of Wisdom literature, with its preference for dialogues and debates (as in Job and in other ancient Near Eastern texts) and for literary forms like "proverb" and "riddle." Speaking, or its more permanent form, writing, is the way wisdom is explicated and taught.

Although the Lord is mentioned by name for the first time in v. 18, it is clear that the poet has been referring to him since the beginning of the chapter. The enemy receives no condemnation; God is the cause of all the trouble. O'Connor (*NIB*) suggests that the withholding of God's name is a literary strategy that avoids blasphemy by not charging God directly with the extreme cruelty described in the first part of the chapter. But the poet of chapter 2 had no such compunctions—the Lord is clearly named as the destroyer in 2:1–2—and there is no reason to think that the poet of chapter 3 was less bold. The literary strategy here is to name God just at the turning point, when, on the one hand, God seems most remote and, on the other hand, just as he is about to become the main topic of the discourse.

The speaker in vv. 18–21 sounds like other biblical sufferers, struggling with themselves in a moment of despair to justify God's harsh actions against them. Compare Ps 77:7–8: "I remember my music at night, with my heart I converse, my spirit searches. Will the Lord spurn forever?" A similar thought appears in Job 10:1 (and cf. 7:11): "I will give free utterance to my complaint, I will speak in the bitterness of my soul." Job goes on to confront God, while the poet of Lamentations tries to excuse him. These verses share words like *zākar, śûaḥ, nepeš, lēb*. The discourse is similar to that of individual laments, but it will move toward wisdom discourse in the next section, to return to individual lament in vv. 43–66. The words "this do I tell myself" in v. 21 refer to what is contained in the following section, the description of the nature of God.

[22–39] As in the book of Job, the assumption in this section is that knowledge of the true nature of God will bring comfort and hope to the sufferer. The speaker reasons with himself as a writer of Wisdom literature might, composing a kind of theodicy.[10] He does not pray or lament, addressing God in the second person, but instead composes an intellectual essay about God, referring to him in the third person and emphasizing abstract concepts like infinity, omnipotence, goodness, and justice. God's loyalty and mercy are infinite, and therefore hope never ends (vv. 22–24, 32). God is good, and the suffering he sends is also good for a person (vv. 25–27). God is just and therefore there must be ample

---

10. The sapiental character of this section has been recognized by earlier scholars, who thought of it as a sermon or as instruction to the community. Westermann, 72, considers vv. 31–38 didactic and midrashic. Few commentators explicate the wisdom aspects of the pericope; an exception is Dobbs-Allsopp (*Lamentations*), who, among other things, notes that vv. 25–39 share the basic outlook of Job's friends.

reason for the suffering he sends; concomitantly, God would not oppress people unfairly (vv. 33–36). God is omnipotent, the source of good and evil, and as long as a person is alive he should accept whatever punishment God metes out to him (vv. 37–39). This is not to say, though, that the theodicy is entirely divorced from the language of prayer, for at several points it invokes liturgical phrases (like the attributes of God) and may even be quoting them, either to use them as support or to refute them.

[22–23] Among the attributes of God are his *ḥesed*, "loyalty," his *raḥămāyw*, "compassion," and his *ʾĕmûnâ*, "faithfulness" (Exod 34:6). It is not unusual to invoke one or more of these attributes in psalms of lament. For example, Ps 88:12–13 calls on God's *ḥesed*, "loyalty," *ʾĕmûnâ*, "faithfulness," and *ṣĕdāqâ*, "justness"—which cannot be invoked by the dead. God's *raḥămîm*, "compassion," refers to God's nature as a merciful God, and his "faithfulness" means his faithfulness to Israel. The sense of *ḥesed* is difficult to convey in English. It means a favor done from a sense of obligation or fidelity, and I have rendered it "acts of loyalty" (it is in the plural in our verse). In the present context, it suggests that God, by virtue of his covenant with Israel, is obligated to help them. More specifically, it may allude to the Davidic covenant (2 Sam 7:15; 1 Kgs 8:23; Isa 55:3; Ps 89:2, and passim), God's unconditional promise to protect the monarchy and its people, even if they sin (Dobbs-Allsopp, *Lamentations*). The poet is insisting, then, that God *must* aid Judah, that it is inconceivable that he would let harm come to the descendants of David, that as long as night follows day God will be faithful to Israel. All that is required is patience (vv. 24–26) and inevitably God will make good on his covenant obligation. Expressions close to this are found in Ps 89, a communal lament that proclaims God's "faithfulness" and "loyalty" (vv. 2–3), that explicitly mentions the Davidic covenant, that speaks of the rejection of God's anointed one, the breaching of walls and the shattering of strongholds, the mockery of passersby, the triumph of the enemy (vv. 39–43), and asks how long God will hide his face (v. 47).

[24] The phrase "My portion is the Lord" resonates in a number of ways. According to Num 18:20, the priests, who had no land allotments, have the Lord as their portion, which means they received their sustenance from the Lord (from offerings brought to the Lord). Just like the priests, the exiles will receive sustenance and protection from God (cf. Pss 16:5; 73:26; 119:57; 142:6) (Hillers). Taking the interpretation one step further, God is the landholding (*ḥēleq*) of Israel in the absence of their physical land (Provan). Our verse would then become the counterpart of Deut 32:9: "The Lord's *ḥēleq* is his people." Another explanation emphasizes that "to have a portion" in a king means to acknowledge his sovereignty (Moskowitz). See 2 Sam 20:1, when Sheba ben Bichri says, "We have no *ḥēleq* in David." In Josh 22:25 and 27 the tribes that settled east of the Jordan risk being thought of as not having a portion in the Lord and insist that this is not so. If we understand the phrase in this sense, the

poet is maintaining that his sovereign is still God, not the Babylonian king. Israel is still God's people, even though they are no longer in the land that God gave to them. Verse 24 reinforces the notion in vv. 22–23 that God and Israel are still bound by their covenant.

[26–30] Forbearance and humility are counseled. Symbols that in other contexts are negative signs of defeat—the yoke (1:14), sitting alone (1:1), putting the mouth in the dust (3:16), the shame of having the cheek struck (Job 17:10)—are here infused with positive meaning. The yoke (v. 27), a symbol of submission, is a metaphor, although its literal meaning comes through in the context of captivity. Jewish tradition views God's commandments as a "yoke," and the phrase is interpreted this way in the Targum.

[28] The phrase "he should sit alone and be still" may also have a link to the trope of death discussed earlier. McDaniel ("Philological Studies, I," 40–42) sees here an elegiac context, partially based on his equation of "put his mouth in the dust" (v. 29) with "lowered their heads to the ground" (2:10). Noting that mourning was a group activity and not something done in isolation, he questions the meaning of "alone" for *bādād*. In the context of mourning, suggests McDaniel, *bādād* may be a synonym of *dmm* II, "to moan, mourn." (See the comment on 2:10.) The phrase would then mean: "He should sit mourning and moaning." McDaniel does not, however, apply this meaning of *bādād* to 1:1, also a context of mourning. While McDaniel's suggested translation of *bādād* is not convincing, he is correct to see the idea of mourning resonating here, along with the more dominant theme of resigned submission. Another way to arrive at this notion is through Anderson's explanation of Isa 6:5 (*Time to Mourn*, 93). Upon hearing the seraphim proclaim "holy, holy, holy," the prophet is silent (*nidmêtî*, from the root *dmh/dmm*) because he feels himself to be in a state of impurity ("a man of impure lips"). If the same idea pertains to our verse, it would mean that the poet, like Isaiah, feels unable to speak before God, since he is in a state of ritual mourning. The gestures of subservience in v. 28 would then take on the aura of mourning.

[31–36] The two aspects of God described in these verses are God as healer and God as the champion of justice. The chapter is most Joblike here, because it, like the book of Job, is inquiring into suffering that appears to be unwarranted and unjustified, in the case of Job because he had not sinned and in the case of Lamentations because God has an eternal and inviolable obligation to protect Judah (vv. 22–24). Just as the poet of Lamentations reasons that it is good to bear God's punishment and that God will heal the pain he inflicted, so Eliphaz tells Job: "See how happy is the man whom God reproves. Do not reject the discipline of the Almighty. He injures, but he binds up; he wounds, but his hands heal" (Job 5:17–18). Likewise, Bildad chides: "Will God pervert the right? Will the Almighty pervert justice?" (Job 8:3). Is the poet of Lam 3 invoking commonly accepted ideas? Does he believe them, like Eliphaz and Bildad, or reject them, like Job?

[37–39] God is all-powerful and all things derive from him, including suffering. The motif of God as creator is a common way to show God's power over everything in the world. Here what is stressed is creation by command (Gen 1 and more poetically in Ps 33:9: "For he spoke and it came into being; he ordered and it stood"). Both good and bad originate from God (cf. Job 2:10 and Isa 45:7). Speech is not only a characteristic of God; in verses that follow, it is speech, in the form of prayer, that is used to call upon God (vv. 55–56); and it is speech in the form of taunts that the enemies used against Israel (vv. 46, 61–63).

Verse 39 is somewhat puzzling. It seems to suggest that it is better to be alive, even with suffering, than to be dead (if this is the sense, it is the antithesis of Job's view). God is showing mercy by keeping a person alive. Moreover, how can he complain about his punishments when they were justified because of his sins? Shlomo Weissbleuth approaches the interpretation from a more rabbinic angle, suggesting that while all is determined by God, humans have free will. If a person sins, it is by his own free will; and thus he has no right to complain about the results of his sin.

[40–66] Despite the valiant attempt at theodicy, reason cannot conquer all. The poem is not an intellectual exercise but a national lament. As the poet struggles to come to terms with the tragedy, his forbearance and hope turn to anger and despair; and the language of wisdom is overwhelmed by the language of lament. If in the preceding section the poet argued that the injustice of the situation demanded that God react with help and compassion, now he argues that God himself is unjust, refusing to accept Judah's contrition. If, earlier, the poet argued that the people must find their error and repent, now he understands that repentance does not automatically lead to forgiveness. What remains is supplication, and in the last part of the chapter the discourse of laments comes to the fore. As a lamenter, the poet can speak more personally once more, and can address God directly and call upon him for help. At times the poet speaks in the name of the people, as he does in vv. 40–47. Then for a few verses he becomes a sad observer (vv. 48–51), and finally, he is the lone victim again (vv. 52–66), as he was at the beginning of the chapter.

[40–44] This section is the theological and poetic turning point. These verses form a transition to a new type of discourse, in which the speaker is "we" instead of "I" and in which God is addressed directly as "you" instead of being spoken about as "he." Furthermore, v. 40 makes the transition from wisdom discourse to lament or penitential psalm. The words *ḥāpāś*, "to search," and *ḥāgar*, "to examine," occur often in wisdom texts (Prov 2:4; 20:27; Job 5:27; 28:3, 27—Westermann, 179), while "return to the LORD" is at home in prayers of supplication. A clear gesture of supplication is the raising of the hands in v. 41.

Most important, these verses constitute a theological turning point. If God is indeed so good and so merciful, and if the people have sinned, the natural next step is that the people must repent and then they will surely be forgiven. But then, like a sudden jolt, comes v. 42, which starkly juxtaposes (without any grammatical conjunction) the admission of the people's sin with God's refusal to forgive. The old theology has proved to be false. Contrary to Jer 18:5–12, which teaches that if the people repent God will change his mind about punishing them, our poet concludes that there is no direct relationship between repentance and forgiveness. This may be the most disturbing idea in the chapter, and in the entire book. The poet does not, however, reject the power of repentance; rather, he implies in the next two verses that repentance would be effective if only it could reach God. That it does not reach him is God's fault. In a masterfully ironic allusion, the poet reinterprets a major religious principle about divine immanence.

The root *skk*, "to cover, veil, shield, screen," which opens vv. 43 and 44, usually has the positive connotation of "to protect from danger." Its most frequent occurrences are in connection with the protecting wings of the cherubs and the *kappōret* (covering) of the ark (Exod 25:20; 37:9; 1 Kgs 8:7; 1 Chr 28:18). The cherubs and the *kappōret* form a kind of lid on top of the ark and they serve as a base for God's throne. This is the place where God is most immanent. The cloud, *ʿānān* (v. 44), has similar associations. It figures in the exodus and the theophany at Sinai (Exod 13:21; 14:19–24; 16:10; 19:16; 33:9–10; Lev 16:2). The cloud pillar in the wilderness leads the people to safety. Psalm 105:39 calls the cloud by which God led the Israelites a protective cover (*māsāk*, from *sākak*). The theophanous cloud, like the ark (which becomes a portable Mt. Sinai), has a dual role: it is the locus of God's revealing himself to the people, and at the same time it serves as a buffer that protects the people from direct contact with the divine, because contact with the divine is dangerous or even fatal. (Even Moses needed to be shielded [*sākak*] from seeing God directly [Exod 33:22].) It is to the cloud pillar and to the cloud of the theophany that vv. 43–44 allude, but with the opposite connotation. Rather than protecting the people as he did from the Egyptians, and leading them to safety, God pursues them and kills them. Rather than sheltering them from the numinous power of the divine, the cloud "protects" God from the people. The vehicle through which God reveals himself here becomes the means by which God keeps himself hidden—a barrier that an angry God has erected to keep out the prayers of the contrite Judeans. This is a devastating negation of a fundamental religious concept inscribed in traditional sources. It is a fierce indictment of God. Nowhere in Lamentations, and perhaps in the entire Bible, is God's refusal to be present more strongly expressed. This is the climax of the poem's theodicy, for at this point the poet reaches a theological impasse.

[48–51] Water is the dominant image in this section, first in the form of tears (vv. 48–51) and then (vv. 53–54) in the form of a cistern in which the poet feels that he is drowning. The motifs are conventional: Ps 69:1–2, 15–16 express the psalmist's fear of drowning; v. 48 echoes Jer 14:17; and v. 49 is similar to the end of Lam 2:18. God looking down from heaven (v. 50) is a common image (Isa 63:15; Pss 14:2; 33:13, and others) and is a partial antidote to God's intentional distancing of himself in vv. 43–44.

Verse 51 is a crux. The words are intelligible but the meaning is anything but transparent, and therefore numerous interpretations and emendations have been offered. The speaker seems to be expressing the extent of his weeping, saying that he has spilled more tears than all the daughters of Jerusalem (i.e., the professional female mourners). For *ʿôlal*, "to do harm," see Lam 1:12, 22; 3:20. I take the *mêm* before *kōl běnôt* as a comparative particle, "more than" (see Moskowitz, 27 n. 38). This differs from the many interpretations that understand the speaker's crying to be *over the fate of the daughters*. An alternative interpretation takes "all the daughters of my city" as meaning the towns of Judah.

[53–55] A cistern is designed to hold water but is also used as a place of imprisonment, and is also the place of death, as in "those that go down to the pit" (Pss 28:1; 30:4; 88:5; 143:7; Prov 1:12). The cistern evokes the story of Joseph, held in a dry cistern, and Jeremiah, imprisoned in a muddy one. But our poet's cistern is full of water and is closed at the top, making it a more dangerous place of confinement. Exilic literature often uses prison (real or metaphoric) as a symbol of exile.[11] So here again there is a nexus between exile and death. Psalm 88:6–7 shares a similar lexicon, the words "I am cut off [from God]" and "deepest cistern."

[55–66] Typical components of psalms of lament appear here: the plea for God to hear the lamenter (vv. 55–57), forensic language—God defending the lamenter (vv. 58–59), the plots and taunts of the enemies (vv. 60–63), and the hope for punishing the enemy (vv. 64–66).

[55–57] The verbs in the perfect tense in vv. 52–66 have been problematic for many commentators. Some take them as an indication of past events that the poet mentions in his present trouble, but I am persuaded by Hillers and by Provan ("Past, Present") that we should understand them as precative perfects. The poet is calling out from present trouble and urging God to heed him. From the cistern of vv. 53–54 he calls out to God, pleading with him to respond. Compare Ps 130.

[58–60] The poet casts himself as a plaintiff in court, calling on God to act as judge in a case in which he is sure he is right and the enemy is wrong. This is reminiscent of Job, but in Job God is the accused as well as the judge; here the accused is the enemy. God is asked to *see* the injustice in this set of verses, and to *hear* it in the next set.

[64–66] Chapters 1–4 end with a note of vengeance, but here the argument is based on justice, not on revenge. If, as the poet has argued, God is just, then

11. D. L. Smith, *The Religion of the Landless*, 171–73.

he must punish those who have acted violently against Israel "for no cause." Our poet does not suggest at this point that the enemy is the vehicle for God's punishment. Rather, he implies that the enemy is no better than Israel and deserves as much punishment. The poet's sense of rightness in the world cannot allow the enemy to flourish. This is part of a broader view that in God's perfect world there is no place for evil. We see this in, for example, Pss 1:6 and 104:35, where the idea of vengeance is entirely absent, but nevertheless, evil people must be dispatched from the world. The poet of chapter 3 wants a return to the world order that pertained before the destruction, for the postdestruction world seems lacking in divine justice.

# Lamentations 4:1–22
# Degradation

א
**1**   Alas, the gold is dulled,
          the purest gold has lost its luster.[a]
      The holy gems are strewn
          at every street corner.[b]

ב
**2**   Zion's precious people,
          worth more than fine gold,
      alas, they were valued as earthen pottery,
          the work of a potter's hands.

ג
**3**   Even jackals[c] offered their teat,
          suckled their cubs.
      My Dear People seem[d] cruel,
          like the ostriches[e] in the wilderness.

ד
**4**   The baby's tongue stuck
          to his palate from thirst.
      Little children begged for bread,
          no one gave them a crumb.

ה
**5**   Those used to feasting on delicacies
          starved in the streets.

Those reared in crimson
huddled in[f] garbage dumps.

ו
6   And my Dear People's punishment has grown larger
than the penalty of Sodom,
which was overthrown in a moment
and no hands were raised against it.

ז
7   Her nobles[g] had been brighter than snow,
whiter than milk,
their bodies had been ruddier than coral,
their physique was sapphire.

ח
8   Their features grew darker than black,
they were unrecognizable in the streets.
Their skin shriveled on their bones,
it became dry as wood.

ט
9   Better off were those slain by the sword
than those slain by famine,
who bleed slowly, stabbed by the lack
of produce from the field.

י
10   With their own hands caring women
cooked their children;
that became their sustenance
in the collapse of my Dear People.

כ
11   The LORD brought his wrath to its peak,
he poured out his hot anger,
And he kindled a fire in Zion
And consumed its foundations.

ל
12   Earthly kings could not believe,
nor any of the world's inhabitants,

that the foe and enemy[h] could enter
the gates of Jerusalem.

ב
**13** On account of the sins of her prophets,
the iniquities of her priests
who shed in her midst
the blood of the righteous.

ג
**14** They wandered blind in the streets,
so befouled with blood
that no one was permitted
to touch their clothing.[i]

ס
**15** "Get away! Impure!" they called out about them,
"Get away, get away! Don't touch!"
as[j] they wandered aimlessly.[k]
They said, "Among the nations
they may no longer reside."[l]

פ
**16** The LORD himself[m] has scattered them;[n]
he no longer looks after them.
The priests were not shown deference,
the elders were not favored.

ע
**17** All the while our eyes wore out[o]
(looking) for our help, for nought,
as we watched and watched[p]
for a nation that could not save.

צ
**18** They stalked[q] our steps
so that we could not walk in our squares.
Our end drew near, our time ran out,
for our end had come.

ק
**19** Swifter were our pursuers
than eagles in the sky.

On the mountains they chased[r] us,
in the wilderness they ambushed us.

ר
**20**   The breath of our life, the LORD's anointed,
was caught in their traps.
The one about whom we said, "In his shade
we will live among the nations."

שׂ
**21**   Rejoice and be glad, Dear Edom,
who dwells in the land of Uz.
To you, too, will come the cup,
you will get drunk and bare yourself.

ת
**22**   Your punishment is completed, Dear Zion.
He will not keep you exiled any longer.
He will attend[s] to your punishment, Dear Edom.
He will expose your sins.

   a. The word *yišneʾ* is written with an *ʾālef* instead of a *hê*; see 2 Kgs 25:29 and Eccl 8:1. The meaning is "to change." A homophonous root means "to gleam," an interpretation preferred by Renkema, who takes it as an adjective modifying "gold" and renders the line, "Ah, how the lustrous gold has grown dim, that pure gold." But this interpretation requires a segmentation of the line that goes against the Masoretic accents and differs from the way most commentators divide it. Renkema's division, however, makes the rhythm 3+2, a *qinah* meter.

   b. Literally, "at the head of every street."

   c. With the Qere. The Kethib is *tânnîn*, "sea serpent," which makes little sense.

   d. The *lāmed* is usually taken as an emphatic particle. Alternatively, the phrase may be construed as having the word *haʿytâ* understood: *bat-ʿammî hayĕtâ lĕ-ʾakzār*, "my Dear People have become cruel."

   e. With the Qere. The usual term for "ostriches" is *bĕnôt yaʿănâ*. Note the assonance between *bat ʿammî* and *[bĕnôt] yaʿănâ*.

   f. *ḥbq*, literally "embraced," here has the sense of "huddle against" or "cling desperately to." Cf. a similar idiom in Job 24:8: *ḥibqû-ṣûr*, "huddled against a rock."

   g. *nĕzîrêhā*, not Nazirites but aristocrats, as in Gen 49:26 and Deut 33:16. (Those who wear a *nēzer*, "crown, wreath.")

   h. *ṣar wĕʾôyēb* may be understood as a hendiadys, "the hostile foe." See also Esth 7:6.

   i. This phrase is barely intelligible. Albrektson (following Budde, Rudolph, and Meek; and accepted in *HALOT* 2:411) takes the subject as the priests and renders: "what they were not allowed, they touched with their clothes." He explains that this means that "those who had been anxious to keep all the cultic rules of purity cannot avoid contact with unclean things." I prefer to understand the subject as the common people (as do several English translations and also O'Connor). The people had to avoid contact with the bloodstained clothing of the priests and prophets, because this clothing was now contaminated and would render impure anyone who touched it. All of this is, of course, a metaphor.

j. *kî* in the sense of "for, as"—a circumstantial clause. The exclamations are uttered while they wander aimlessly. The wandering is not a result of the declaration of impurity (as many translations have it) but concomitant with it. The notice of the wandering began in the previous verse and is continued here.

k. The word *nāṣû* is difficult. It may be related to "feathers" (Lev 1:16), hence "take flight." More likely it comes from *nwṣ,* "to distance oneself, flee," or perhaps *nṣh,* "to go to ruin." Most translations take it as a synonym for *nāʿû,* "to wander," as I have. I have translated the two words as a hendiadys.

l. I have followed Hillers in segmenting this line slightly differently from most translations. This segmentation makes more sense grammatically, since it accounts better for the preposition *b-* and does not leave *lāgûr* without an indirect object (supplied in many translations by the addition of the word "here"). Others read: "They say among the nations: 'They may not live here any longer." I interpret the subject of "they said" as the same impersonal subject who "called out" in the first part of the verse.

m. Literally, "the face of the LORD." Perhaps his angry face, as in Lev 26:17; cf. also Ps 34:17; or simply referring to God as in Exod 33:15 (Moskowitz).

n. For *ḥillāgām* in this sense see Gen 49:7.

o. For *tiklênâ ʿênênû* see F. J. Helfmeyer, "*kālâ,*" *TDOT* 7:163–64. The idiom means "to long for something, to wait anxiously" (see Lam 2:11). In this case, it is more concrete than just an idiom for longing, since the idea of looking for a long, long time is repeated in the next part of the verse. One can imagine the lookouts of the city watching from the ramparts for help to arrive. See the following note.

p. Literally, "in our watching we watched." Rather than taking the noun as a gerund, NIV (following Albrektson and others) renders "from our towers [i.e., 'our watching places'] we watched."

q. Hunted, from *sûd* or *ṣādâ.*

r. For *dālag* meaning "to pursue, chase," see Gen 31:36; 2 Sam 17:53; Ps 10:2.

s. The verbs are in the perfect tense, as if the poet, like a prophet, sees these actions as already completed.

## Commentary

While chapter 3 can be seen as a portrayal of the exile from the perspective of an individual, chapter 4 focuses on the community and its experience of the siege. Like chapter 3, this chapter contains physical description, but with a different slant. Whereas chapter 3 described the brutality of battle and the toll on the body of the march into exile, chapter 4 documents the physical changes wrought by the starvation of the siege: the throats slaked with thirst (v. 4), the blackened faces and shriveled skin (v. 8), the blinded eyes (v. 14), the eyes worn out from watching (v. 17), the slowed steps (v. 18).

As the descriptions progress, we relive, step by step, the siege and its accompanying suffering. Yet, because the images are for the most part conveyed by a third-person observer, there is an odd sense of detachment, amplified by the contrast between what was before and what is now, and the contrast between a normal society and the abnormal conditions that characterize the siege. We thus become voyeurs, watching in horror as the sequence of events unfolds.[1] These events are played out in an urban landscape, for in a siege no one can leave the city.

The main theme of this chapter is degradation: everything beautiful has been sullied, things of priceless value are treated as if worthless. Precious and beautiful objects are metaphors for the most precious things—human beings. People who were like gold, like precious gems, have become as worthless as potsherds (vv. 1–2); the elite, accustomed to delicacies, are reduced to eating garbage (v. 5); society's leaders, once as magnificent as coral and sapphire, have turned into dried-up wood, abject figures, shrivelled from hunger (vv. 7–8). The picture is not only one of heartrending snapshots of individuals in their misery, but of the abrogation of all that was normal in Judean society, a drastic reversal of fortunes, socially and physically, caused by the ravages of wartime famine. The rich have become destitute, the leaders are powerless, and activities normally pursued in the privacy of one's home are done in full public view on the streets—all human dignity has been lost.

The cause of the degradation is the famine of the siege, and its effects are described in a realistic sequence in which starvation weakens the population: first the children, who are starving (vv. 3–4); then the adults, whose health deteriorates precipitously (vv. 5–8); then the ultimate trope for starvation: cannibalism (v. 10). Studies of famine note that the most vulnerable are children beyond the time of nursing. Children who are nursed have a somewhat lesser mortality rate, but nursing is very demanding on the mother and it is extremely difficult for her body to meet the extra nutritional demands. Adults do not die as quickly, as v. 9 is painfully aware, and when they do it is often because of disease brought on by malnutrition and unsanitary conditions.

Despite the realism of the sequence, this is a poetic rendition of the conditions of famine. This chapter is the most graphic in the book in its description of the physical suffering of the people of Jerusalem, and what makes it especially vivid is the use of color. In fact, color is one of the striking features of the

---

1. Several recent exegetes, notably Hillers, O'Connor, and Dobbs-Allsopp, have recognized what I call the sense of distance, but they have interpreted in different ways. I do not find "a sense of remoteness and exhaustion" as O'Connor does, nor do I think, with Dobbs-Allsopp, that there is a diminution of emotion or a matter-of-factness in this chapter. The more objective or distant stance of this chapter yields a poem no less moving, and indeed, one that is more graphic, than the earlier chapters. It is simply employing a different literary vehicle.

chapter: gold and scarlet (vv. 1, 2, 5), white, red, sapphire, black (vv. 7, 8). Bright colors represent the earlier conditions; as the famine progresses, the colors are erased from the picture and all that remains is dullness and blackness.

Another dimension evoked in the chapter is heat, which one can almost feel through the mention of the dry and blackened skin (v. 8), the parched mouths (v. 4), and God's burning anger setting fire to Zion (v. 11). This is the siege of summer: the time of rainlessness, of baking sun and unrelenting heat. There is no shade, no protection from God or king (v. 20).

And so there is no escape from the inevitable destruction. God does not look at the people or answer them (v. 16). The enemy is at the gate, nay, breaking through the gate, pursuing the citizens of Jerusalem in the city squares as well as outside in the mountains and deserts as they try to flee (vv. 18–19). The unimaginable is played out before our eyes, even as the eyes of the besieged grow weary looking for help.

The explanation for the tragedy is expressed in terms of the purity paradigm (see Introduction). The priests and prophets have become morally impure by shedding blood (a symbol of idolatry), a sin that defiles the land and leads to exile. Their impurity is represented metaphorically as the ritual impurity of the leper, a condition that prevents contact with the holy—an ironic touch since it is the priests and the prophets whose professional domain was God's teaching (Torah) and his revelation (God's word; cf. Jer 18:18). The priests and prophets are a metonym for the people ("a kingdom of priests," Exod 19:6), who are rejected and scattered by God. Despite its focus on devastation, the chapter ends with a ray of hope, mixed with the desire for revenge. "Wait," says the poet, "you may gloat now, Edom, but your turn for punishment will come shortly." Thus the poem that began by describing the reversal of Judah's beauty and vigor ends by envisioning the same reversal for its enemy. As Judah's punishment draws to an end, Edom's punishment will begin.

Chapter 4 returns to a single alphabetic acrostic, and, like chapters 1 and 2, opens with the word *ʾêkâ*. The verses are shorter than those in the first two chapters but longer than the verses in chapter 3.

**[4:1–2]** The image begins with the debasement of what seems at first to be the precious objects in the temple (v. 1), but soon turns into a metaphor for Zion's people weakened by starvation (v. 2). These precious objects have become worthless and disposable. Three different words for "gold" are used. Gold is a symbol of great value and permanence, but here its value is diminished, its luster is dulled. Hillers's objection that gold does not tarnish, and that therefore an emendation is required, misses the mark; this gold is dulled from dirt, not from tarnish. It is not that the gold itself has gone bad, but that the treatment it has received has ruined it. In a similar vein, the *holy gems* (*ʾabnê qōdeš*, literally "holy stones") evokes the temple structure or its decorative objects, or even perhaps the temple vessels or the priestly ephod and breastplate, which were set with precious stones (Exod 28). While it is possible that ʾabnê qōdeš is an idiom that means simply "gems," not "holy gems," the word "holy" is part of the connotation of the phrase, especially as we realize that the reference is to Israel, a "holy nation" (Exod 19:6), a nation reserved especially for God (Ps 114:2).[2]

Precious things that are normally kept secure in private places are now "strewn [literally, 'poured out'] at every street corner," that is, dumped in public places where anyone can see and take them. The streets and squares, that is, public domains, often figure in Lamentations as the places where people languish and die (2:11, 12, 19, 21; 4:5, 8, 14). This is, of course, a reversal of the norm, and not unlike the grim picture of homelessness in many modern U.S. cities.

In contrast to gold and gems, earthen pots were cheap and common, and broken pieces of pottery (sherds) were often scattered about. The idea is that human beings, far more precious than fine gold, have become "throwaway" objects. For broken pottery metaphors see Isa 30:14; Jer 48:12. A similar image occurs in the Lamentation over the Destruction of Sumer and Ur (Michalowski, *Lamentation*, 63), line 406: "In Ur (people) were smashed as if they were clay pots." The addition in v. 2 of "the work of a potter's hands" is not merely for clarification. It evokes a set of associations in which God is to Israel as a potter is to his pottery. In the creation story God, in forming the first human from earth (clay), is imagined as a potter (Gen 2:7). The prophets develop the metaphor: the people are like pottery vis-à-vis God, the divine potter (Isa 64:7), who can reshape his people whenever he chooses (Jer 18:6), and the clay pot cannot question what the potter makes (Isa 45:9). The pottery is frail and helpless. The message is clear: the people have been degraded into the cheapest and least permanent material and have no control over what becomes of them. Dobbs-Allsopp (*Lamentations*) goes even further, imagining Jerusalem littered with the bodies of dead children instead of pottery, or with dead children among the sherds.

The reality that stands behind these metaphors is the lessening of the value of people during a siege, especially slaves and children. Children, considered a blessing and normally valued for their economic contributions to the family and for the family's continuity, become a liability during a siege because they must be fed and cared for. In some cases, children were sold so that they could receive care from others.[3]

In v. 2 "Zion's people" (Heb. běnê ṣiyyôn, literally "Zion's children") is a poetic term, not a sociological one. It personifies the people (not only the residents of Jerusalem but the nation as a whole) as the children of Mother Zion (cf. Ps 149:2; Joel 2:23).[4] Some translations render "children of Zion," implying that

---

2. J. A. Emerton, "The Meaning of ʾabnê-qōdeš in Lamentations 4:1," *ZAW* 79 (1967): 233–36.
3. Ephʿal, *Siege*, 104.
4. For Zion as a mother see Frymer Kensky, *In the Wake of the Goddesses*, 176.

the reference is to actual children; but this is an overly narrow interpretation, and it is preferable to understand the term more broadly as meaning the people. The chapter is concerned with both adults and children, and both are mentioned in the verses that follow.

[3–4] These verses highlight the children, and compare the care that the human children receive with that of the least pleasant animal offspring. Jackals and ostriches occur together as an associated pair (Isa 34:13; Mic 1:8; Job 30:29) and share the characteristics of inhabiting ruins and uttering eerie cries that sound like keening. Like jackals and ostriches, Zion's people preside over a ruin. The conventional use of these two animals is augmented by their use to show the inability of the human mothers to feed their children, which is the point of this verse. The Judean mothers are contrasted with jackals, who, although thought of as despicable animals, at least suckle their offspring, and they are compared to ostriches, who were believed to abandon their eggs (Job 39:13–17). Whereas our poet invokes wild animals, the Annals of Ashurbanipal refer to domesticated animals in the portrait of starvation: "Even when the camel foals, the donkey foals, calves or lambs were suckling many times . . . on the mother animals, they could not fill their stomachs with milk" (*ANET*, 300).

The inability of parents to nurture their children, as described in v. 3, culminates in the children's starvation, portrayed graphically in v. 4. The infant is so parched with thirst that he cannot even suck, or, more poignantly, cannot cry. The expression "tongue sticking to the roof of the mouth" occurs in Ezek 3:26; Job 29:10; and Ps 137:6, and in all cases it signals the inability to make sounds. (The idea of "dried up" is expressed in a slightly different idiom in Ps 22:16: "my vigor is dried up like a shard; and my tongue is stuck to my gums [*malqôḥāy*].") The infants are so weak from starvation that they no longer cry when hungry. There may be an implied contrast with v. 3 in that the jackal and ostrich are known for the sounds they make, while in v. 4 the infants can make no sound. Children beyond the age of suckling beg for food, but "no one gives them a crumb." Hebrew *pōrēś/pōrēs* means both "to extend, spread out," and "to break bread," and both meanings are in play here.

[5] Verse 5 may continue the description of the children's condition, but it seems more likely that it refers to the adults, specifically those of the upper class. Not only can they not provide for their children, they cannot even provide for themselves. Their former luxury contrasts sharply with their current deprivation. "Crimson" (*tôlāʿ*) is an unusual word associated with the color red (Isa 1:18) and was perhaps a pigment manufactured from a certain worm. The brightly colored and presumably expensive clothing contrasts with their owners' now destitute state. To huddle in garbage dumps is one step worse than lying in the streets; it means to live in the squalor of dire poverty (1 Sam 2:8; Ps 113:7). Hillers's translation "pick through garbage" is evocative of the modern urban homeless, a rough parallel to what our verse pictures; but the garbage dump is not the

source of food, it is where the people live. The verse is not only describing the lack of food, but the total reversal in the standard of living, from highest luxury to direst poverty. Compare the curse in the Treaty of Aššur-nerariv with Mati'- ilu, king of Arpad (rev. IV, 14–16): "May dust be their food, pitch their ointment, donkey's urine their drink, papyrus their clothing, and may their sleeping place be in the dung heap."[5]

[6–10] The siege, viewed as a punishment for Judah's sin, is described in terms of a reversal from former glory and in terms of being slow and drawn out. Sodom, the archetypical image of corruption and destruction (see Isa 1:9–10), was destroyed instantaneously, with no suffering leading up to the destruction (Gen 19:23–25). Jerusalem, by contrast, had to suffer a protracted siege before being destroyed, making Jerusalem's destruction worse than Sodom's. Moreover, no human enemy besieged and destroyed Sodom (the apparent meaning of "no hands were raised against it"), whereas Jerusalem suffered extended enemy attacks, suggesting another way in which Jerusalem's fate was worse than Sodom's. Two synonyms, *ʿāwôn* and *ḥaṭṭāʾt*, are used, and both can mean "sin" or "punishment." Here "punishment" and "penalty" are more apt than "sin," but the echo of "sin" is not entirely absent.

[7–8] These verses play on the reversal of the people's health, using color and its absence. The description of the former physical well-being of the upper classes imitates the *wasf* in Song 5:10–15. Their complexion was clear and healthy, their bodies strong. The description is made in terms of colors signifying radiant health and beauty: white and red—as in the description of the lover in Song 5:10—and sapphire. For the word *ʿeṣem* (literally, "bone") in the sense of "body" see Prov 16:24. The more difficult term *gizrâ* ("physique") may refer either to the physique (the form) or, less likely, to the face. My sense is that *ʿeṣem* and *gizrâ* are meant to refer not to specific parts of the body, but to the general look of the person. The last element of the description, *sappîr gizrātām*, has been interpreted as either "their hair was sapphire" or "their stature was sapphire." Many modern commentators point to the statues of Mesopotamian kings, in which hair and beards were designated by inlays of lapis lazuli, and understand our phrase as a borrowing of this image. The meaning is that their hair was shining—another sign of good health, like the other elements in the verse. My preference is to accept the meaning that their form or stature—their physique—was shining or splendid. I have chosen this interpretation (as has Renkema) as a better parallel with *ʿeṣem*, "bones, body, figure." In either case,

5. Parpola and Watanabe, *Neo-Assyrian Treaties and Loyalty Oaths,* 11. The term for dung heap is *tubkinu* and is translated in *ANET,* 533, as "corners (of walls)." Similar motifs are found in the Lamentation over the Destruction of Sumer and Ur, line 304: "The king who was used to eating marvelous food grabbed at a (mere) ration" (Michalowski, *Lamentation,* 55); and in the Curse of Agade, lines 249–53: "May your aristocrats, who eat fine food, lie (hungry) in the grass" (Cooper, *Curse of Agade,* 63).

the picture is one of radiant good health. "Sapphire" connotes "brilliant, shiny, sparkling, of good color" (cf. Exod 24:10; Ezek 1:26). The choice of this word adds to the palette of colors in this verse.

The Atra-hasis Epic contains a parallel description of the effects of prolonged famine.

> When the third year came,
> Their looks were changed by starvation,
> Their faces covered with scabs (?) like malt,
> They stayed alive by . . . life.
> Their faces looked sallow,
> They went out in public hunched,
> Their well-set shoulders slouched,
> Their upstanding bearing bowed.[6]

The use of color to describe the former state of the people in v. 7 is in stark contrast to what has become of them (v. 8). Their faces and bodies are now blackened—that is, all the color is erased from them, all their radiance is gone. Compare the curse in Esarhaddon's Succession Treaty, line 585: "May they make your flesh and the flesh of your brothers, your sons and your daughters as black as [bitu]men, pitch and naphtha."[7] Now the people are completely changed, beyond recognition, by the ravages of famine. They are burned up, shriveled, literally dehydrated. (See also 5:10 for flesh charred from famine.) Instead of being compared to jewels, they are compared to wood, dry and dull, a cheap commodity. The comparison to wood reflects the reality of starvation in which the skin of the starving person becomes pale, dry, and less elastic.

[9–10] These verses sum up the toll of the suffering in physical pain and familial relationships. Verse 9 echoes the idea of the protracted suffering also present in v. 6. A quick death in battle is preferable to the slow and agonizing death from starvation. The effects of famine are equated metaphorically to wounds, from which the lifeblood drains out slowly (cf. 2:12). The wording of the second half of the verse is somewhat difficult. *yāzûbû měduqqārîm* means literally "they flow out, pierced." The *mem* before *těnûbōt* is a separative *mem*, meaning "without the produce of the field." Thus they are pierced by the lack of food.

While the metaphor is striking, there may be a reference to a real-life phenomenon. Herman Vanstiphout finds a similar image in the Lamentation over the Destruction of Ur, line 225, which says: "those afflicted by the Weapon, the Weapon did kill." Although most Sumerologists see here a reference to battle, Vanstiphout tentatively suggests that this is a reference to bubonic plague, one

---

6. Atra-hasis II, iv. Translated in Stephanie Dalley, *Myths from Mesopotamia* (Oxford: Oxford University Press, 1991), 22–23. A similar description occurs repeatedly in Atra-hasis.

7. Parpola and Watanabe, *Neo-Assyrian Treaties and Loyalty Oaths*, 64.

of whose symptoms is subcutaneous bleeding that has the appearance of wounds. These black markings are apparently the origin of the term "Black Death."[8] This interpretation of the Sumerian lament is questionable, but the suggestion of bubonic plague may fit the description of blackened features and being stabbed by famine in vv. 8–9. Verse 5 mentions living in garbage dumps, and the loss of health in vv. 8–9 is the natural consequence.

Verse 10 returns to the idea of mothers and children (see v. 3), but with a stronger, more wrenching image. The trope of cannibalism (see commentary on 2:20) is made more horrible by the adjective "caring, compassionate" (*raḥămā-nîyôt*). The contrast between the mothers' normal behavior and their current actions become all the more vivid. For *lĕbārôt*, "sustenance," see 2 Sam 13:5, 7, 10. The phrase *šeber bat-ʿammî*, "collapse of my Dear People," occurs in 2:11 and 3:48 (also Jer 8:11, 21). Here it creates an ironic play on words, for in addition to meaning "collapse," *šeber* also means "food/grain provisions" (e.g., Gen 42:1–2). Moreover, an ironic echo of the image of birthing—the words *reḥem* ("womb") and *mašbēr* ("birthstool"—2 Kgs 19:3; Isa 37:3; Hos 13:13) may be felt through the words *raḥămāniyyôt* and *šeber*.

[11–16] The tone in this section becomes more theological, as God is mentioned for the first time. He is the source of this disaster, which is a punishment for Judah's sins. Shockingly, God has permitted the enemy to enter his inviolate sanctuary; and he has held the religious leaders, priests and prophets, responsible for the people's sins. The result, in v. 16, is that the people are exiled and God no longer shows concern for them.

The phrase in v. 11, "The LORD brought his wrath to its peak" (literally "used up [*killâ*] his wrath") makes a nice contrast with 3:22: "his compassion is not used up." Surely, no greater divine wrath could be imagined than that which caused Jerusalem's destruction. As for God's compassion, its infiniteness offers the basis for hope. Isaiah 54:7–8 invokes the idea of the briefness of God's anger and the everlastingness of his compassion as part of his message of comfort.

God's anger is hot, it burns like a fire (Ezek 22:31; Hos 8:5; Nah 1:6; Zeph 3:8, and elsewhere), and here it sets the city ablaze. Destruction by fire is a common image in prophetic literature and elsewhere (see Lam 1:13 and 2:4) and is a figurative way of saying that God's judgment will pour down on a city. The prototype of destruction by fire is Sodom (Gen 19:24), already invoked in v. 6 in a different context. Even closer to the theological outlook of Lamentations is Deuteronomy, where we read: "lest the anger of the LORD your God blaze forth against you and he destroy you from the face of the earth" (Deut 6:15). While the image of destruction by fire is a metaphor, there is a bit of realia behind it. Cities were set on fire in war, and this often marked the final stage of their conquest.

8. "The Death of an Era," 87.

The reaction of outsiders (v. 12) serves a similar literary purpose as the mocking of passersby in 2:15–16 in that it reinforces the idea from a different perspective. Here the entire world is amazed that Jerusalem's security could be breached, as the shock of the people of Judah is displaced onto the hypothetical kings and citizens of the world. In other words, everyone is made to side with Judah in its amazement that the unthinkable has occurred. Needless to say, in reality other nations would not be the least surprised that Jerusalem was destroyed by the Babylonian Empire. This idea expresses the Judean theological perspective of the inviolability of Jerusalem (see, e.g., 2 Sam 7:11–16; Ps 48:3–6), namely, that God would not permit his city, the site of his temple and the capital of the Davidic monarchy, to come to harm. Indeed, the disbelief of the foreign kings at Jerusalem's fall may be an inversion of Ps 48:5–6—the amazement of kings at the splendor of Jerusalem. Obviously, the view of Jerusalem's inviolability is challenged by the destruction of Jerusalem, although Lamentations does not attempt to address the challenge. Instead, it uses this theology to underscore quite dramatically the religious and psychological impact of the destruction.

[13–15] These verses provide an explanation for the destruction, which seemed so incredible to the onlookers in v. 12. The explanation calls on the purity paradigm, wherein exile is explained as a consequence of impurity (see Introduction). The priests and prophets—the same leaders whose deaths were decried in 2:20—are here accused of having caused the catastrophe. These "holy" officials, closely associated with God's Torah and the ongoing revelation of his word (Jer 18:18), are the ones expected to be most pure. But they have become morally impure, for they have "shed the blood of the righteous." The accusation of shedding blood is a cipher for idolatry, and need not be taken literally. Similar language linking bloodshed and idolatry occurs in Ezek 22:1–5 and Ps 106:37–40. Idolatry, like bloodshed, renders the land impure and leads to the exile of the people. There is also an echo of the story of Cain (Gen 4:10–12), where Cain, the murderer, is forced to become a wanderer. Here vv. 14–15 argue implicitly that through the perversity of the priests and prophets the people of Judah have become defiled (through idolatry), and this has led to their destruction and exile.

Bloodshed and idolatry are forms of moral impurity, but the poet goes one step further and metaphorically represents this moral impurity as ritual impurity—in this case the ritual impurity of the leper. Just as the leper may not come in contact with the holy, so the priests and the prophets are cut off from contact with God. Moreover, like the leper, they are pariahs in their own society and are shunned by the people. Like the priests and prophets, Judah too has become a pariah among the nations in that she has lost her place among the nations of the world. This same idea can be found in Lam 1:1, which contains the phrase *yāšĕbâ bādād*, an echo of Lev 13:46, which says of the leper: *hû ᵓ bādād yēšēb*, "he will live apart."

The blind wanderers of v. 14 are the priests and prophets of v. 13, befouled by the blood they have spilled. A similar association of ideas and images occurs in Zeph 1:17. There is a certain irony in prophets—visionaries—being blind. While the spilled blood is primarily a metaphor for idolatry, we should not eliminate its possible association with the actual blood of the victims of war. That is, the priests and prophets have, through their improper actions, caused people to be killed in the war. Compare the Targum's explanation of the blood as "the blood of those slain by the sword."

The second part of v. 14 is only partially intelligible, and has prompted a range of emendations and interpretations, none of which has been unanimously accepted. I understand the scene to be one in which the priests and prophets are (figuratively) soiled with the blood that they have shed, and that therefore others cannot touch their clothing, lest they, too, be rendered impure. Ancient interpreters, exemplified by the LXX and Targum, took a different line of interpretation of the first part of the verse by dissociating the blind from the priests and prophets. According to these ancient versions, the blind, because they could not see, mistakenly touched the bloody garments of the priests and prophets.

In v. 15 the priests and prophets are likened in their impurity to lepers. They are impure (morally) from having spilled the blood of the innocent just as lepers are impure ritually. Whereas the leper himself must ordinarily proclaim his state of impurity to warn away others (Lev 13:45: "he [the leper] shall call out: 'Impure, Impure'"), here members of the public warn others that a "leper" is near and that they (the public) should keep their distance so as not to come in physical contact with him. It is possible to see these words coming from the mouth of the impure, as Gordis does, but the exclamation is more effective, I think, coming from the mouths of the onlookers.

In the last part of the verse, the metaphor fades into its literal referent: the people of Judah. The phrase is usually rendered: "They say among the nations, 'They shall stay here no longer.'" But this translation suggests at best, as Provan explains, that the people of Zion are pictured as living in the midst of the community of nations as sojourners and that now they are being asked to leave. This interpretation makes little sense. It is better to understand that Judah, like the leper, is a pariah among its neighbors. In the world of nations, Judah no longer has a rightful place. The subject of "say" is the same unidentified voice that "called out" earlier in the verse. These verbs are impersonal and could be rendered as "it was called out, it was said." Our verse ends with *baggôyim gûr*, "reside among the nations." Similar but not identical expressions are found in 1:3: *yāšbâ baggôyim*, "dwell among the nations," and 4:20: *niḥyeh baggôyim*, "live among the nations." It is not clear if these expressions have different nuances.

Isaiah 52:11 alludes to and reverses the image in our verse: "Get away, get away, get out of there: Impure, don't touch." In Isa 52 it is Babylonia, not Judah, who is impure; and Judah will distance herself from the impurity of Babylonia as a person distances himself from a leper.[9]

[17–20] The discourse shifts to first-person plural as the surviving community describes the final stages of Jerusalem's fall. Alternatively, one may interpret this shift in voice as the speaker's move from being an objective observer to being a member of the Judean community. The besieged population waited and waited for help to come from another nation, but none did. Time ran out and the enemy finally entered the city. The description in these verses may be illuminated by the account in 2 Kgs 25. Some people were able to escape from the city, but were pursued wherever they ran (to the mountains and wilderness, or perhaps "the mountainous wilderness," according to v. 19, which may be the Arabah, the desert steppe east of Jerusalem, mentioned in 2 Kgs 25:5). King Zedekiah was among those who escaped, but he was captured near Jericho. His sons were executed in front of him and his eyes were then put out, and he was led in chains to Babylon. These events, recorded in 2 Kgs 25:1–7, mark the nadir of the royal house of Judah, the symbol of the nation: Zedekiah, physically maimed, has lost his heirs to the throne and hence the dynasty, and is led away as a prisoner into exile. Second Kings does not end its account at this point, but concludes on a positive note with the exiled King Jehoiachin alive and well in Babylon, being accorded royal privileges. Second Kings holds out hope for the continuation of the dynasty. Lamentations 4, however, holds out no such hope, ending with the king's (Zedekiah's) capture. This chapter that began with the degradation of the "precious gems" ends with the degradation of the royal house.

The section is marked by a contrast between the passiveness and motionlessness of the besieged population, who wait helplessly, unable even to walk about in the public squares (vv. 17–18), and the swiftness and aggressiveness of the enemy as they pursue the escapees (v. 19). The Judeans are stalked and caught like trapped animals, while the enemy fly like eagles over wild terrain (mountains and wilderness).

[17] The refusal to give up hope in a hopeless situation conveys, in the hindsight perspective of the speaker, a political naïveté. It is interesting to note that this hope is couched in political terms rather than in religious terms; that is, the hope was for deliverance from another nation, not from God. Although the reference may be general, it could refer to a concrete expectation. Some scholars, pointing to Jer 37:5–10, see a veiled reference to Egypt as the nation from whom help was expected (Hillers, Moskowitz, and others). The reference to Egypt becomes even more likely if our verse is an allusion to Isa 30:7, which uses the word *hebel* ("for nought") together with *ʿēzer* ("help") of Egypt. Provan notes that the only nation mentioned by name in the book is Edom, and he prefers to

---

9. See Sommer, *Prophet*, 272 n. 55; and Willey, *Remember*, 126–27.

connect the failed helper of this verse with the condemnation of Edom in v. 22. He also raises the question of whether the nation *could* not or *would* not save Judah, that is, whether it was unable to render help or refused to do so. The Hebrew does not permit this distinction; the phrase *gôy lōʾ yôšiaʿ* simply means "a nonsaving nation."

[20] Most commentators take this verse as referring to Zedekiah. "The breath of our life" is the person upon whom the people's lives depend. "The LORD's anointed" is the king belonging to the Davidic dynasty. Gerstenberger hesitates to see this as a reference to the flight of Zedekiah and suggests instead that this verse may attest to a more developed concept of a future messiah, but that seems unlikely.

The recollection of what had previously been said of the king, that "in his shade we will live among the nations," may be a reference to Zedekiah's rebellion against Babylonia. Though rousing high hopes (Jer 28), it proved to be a disaster. Shade or shadow is a common metaphor for protection; for its use in terms of the protection of countries or rulers, that is, political protection, see Isa 30:3; 32:2. While the blinding of Zedekiah is not mentioned specifically, the emphasis on blindness in v. 14 and worn-out eyes in v. 17 might be veiled references to it.

[21–22] The concluding verses contain a sardonic address to Edom to rejoice at Judah's demise. Anderson (*Time to Mourn*, 94) sees here more than simple happiness at an enemy's trouble; he puts it in the context of ritual mourning on an international scale. Not only did Edom fail to comfort Judah, she laughed at her misery—a breach of covenant fidelity for which she would pay a price. "Dear Edom" is paralleled with "Dear Zion"—they will soon switch places, Edom to suffer punishment and Zion to be released from hers.

Edom personifies the enemy, as in Ps 137:7, where the word *ʿr,* "strip/bare," also occurs in the context of the punishment. The history of the relations between Edom and Judah are complex and not altogether known. Edom became a vassal of Babylonia under Nebuchadnezzar (after 605 B.C.E.), but whether it aided Babylonia in its conquest of Judah is uncertain. Clearly, though, in the prophetic writings, Edom is a traditional enemy—cf. Isa 34:5–17; 63:1–6; Ezek 25:12–14; 35:3–15; Joel 4:19; Obadiah; Mal 1:2–5.[10] Edom is synonymous with Esau (Gen 36:1), and is thus the symbol of an ancient and perpetual rival to Israel. For the link between Edom and Uz, see Gen 36:28 and 1 Chr 1:42–43. Edom as a code word for the enemy continues beyond the period of the Hebrew Bible. First Esdras 4:45 blames Edom for the burning of the temple when Judea was laid waste by the Chaldeans (see also *1 Enoch* 89:66). In the rabbinic tradition after the destruction of the Second Temple, Edom stands for Rome.

---

10. See J. R. Bartlett, *Edom and the Edomites,* 151–61; and idem, "Edom and the Fall of Jerusalem 587 B.C.," *PEQ* 114 (1982): 13–24.

The cup of God's wrath, from which the wicked "drink" their divine punishment, seems to have been a familiar motif. It occurs in Jer 25:15–29, where many nations are mentioned, including "all the kings of the land of Uz" (but not the name Edom). The cup of wrath also figures in Isa 51:17, 22; Jer 49:12; 51:7; Ezek 23:31–34; Ps 75:9; and, along with drunkenness and nakedness, in Hab 2:15–16. (Cf. also Gen 9:21–22 for drunkenness leading to nakedness.)

Drinking from the cup of wrath is associated with getting drunk, which is, in turn, associated with nakedness and shame. Edom, personified as a woman, thereby has female sexual shame attached to her, as Jerusalem did in chapter 1. Edom will bare her body, and God will expose her sins. The enemy is now the immoral woman while Zion's sins have been paid for and she is once again virtuous. (Compare Isa 40:2 for the idea that Zion's punishment has been completed.)

The ending of our chapter resembles the ending of Joel 4, according to which Egypt and Edom will be destroyed and Judah will be forever inhabited. This is the most hopeful note in the entire book of Lamentations.

# Lamentations 5:1–22
# Prayer

1     Consider, LORD, what has become of us,
      look and see our degradation.

2     Our ancestral land has been turned over to outsiders,
      our households to foreigners.

3     We have become orphans, fatherless;
      our mothers are widows.[a]

4     We have to pay for our drinking water,
      our firewood comes at a price.

5     At our necks we are pursued.
      We are exhausted, and there is no let up.

6     To Egypt we extended our hand,
      to Assyria, to furnish food.

7     Our fathers sinned and are no more,
      and we suffer their punishments.

8     Slaves rule over us,
      there is no release from their hand.

9     With our lives in peril we get bread
      in the face of the desertlike drought.

| 10 | Our skin was inflamed[b] like an oven, |
| | by the famine's searing blast. |
| 11 | Women were raped in Zion, |
| | maidens in the cities of Judah. |
| 12 | Princes were hung up by their hands, |
| | elders received no respect. |
| 13 | Youths pulled the millstone, |
| | and boys staggered under wood-loads. |
| 14 | Elders have gone from the gate, |
| | youths from their melodies. |
| 15 | The joy of our heart has gone, |
| | our rejoicing has been turned into mourning. |
| 16 | The crown has fallen from our head; |
| | woe are we, for we have sinned. |
| 17 | Because of this our heart has languished, |
| | because of these our eyes are dulled, |
| 18 | because of Mount Zion, so desolate |
| | that foxes roam around on it.[c] |
| 19 | You, LORD, are enthroned forever, |
| | your throne is everlasting. |
| 20 | Why do you eternally ignore us, |
| | forsake us our whole life long? |
| 21 | Take us back, LORD, to yourself; O let us come back. |
| | Make us again as we were before.[d] |
| 22 | But instead[e] you reject us completely, |
| | you are angry with us, so very much. |

a. The *kāp* before *ʾalmānôt* is asseverative; see the comment on 1:20.

b. The verb *nikmārû* is plural, although the subject, "our skin," is singular. Perhaps the plural suffix, "our," influenced the verb. The exact translation of *nikmārû* is uncertain. LXX renders "has become black and blue," Peshitta "shriveled," Targum "has become darkened," and the Vulgate "is burned up." Modern exegetes defend a similar range of meanings. The problem is that the Hebrew term is rare (only in Gen 43:30; 1 Kgs 3:26; Hos 11:8—all in connection with emotions) and that the comparison to an oven may refer to its color (dark or black, or glowing red), to heat or scorching, or to the shriveling or cracking that heat produces. It is not clear if this phrase is similar in meaning to the blackening of the complexion in 4:8. If so, "charred" or "scorched" would be better translations.

c. I have taken a small syntactic liberty in translating this phrase in order to better capture its meaning. A more literal translation is: "Because of Mount Zion, which is desolate; foxes roam around on it."

d. Literally, "Renew our days as in earlier times."

e. On the restrictive sense ("rather") of *kî ʾim* see Waltke and O'Connor, *Biblical Hebrew Syntax,* 671.

## Commentary

The opening words mark chapter 5 as a prayer, and indeed some Greek and Latin manuscripts contain the superscription "A prayer," "A prayer of Jeremiah," or "A prayer of Jeremiah the prophet." The chapter calls on God to notice the abject state of the people—the disintegration of their personal and communal lives—and to restore them to their former condition. It resembles in part the communal laments in the book of Psalms and shares some traits with penitential prayers of the Second Temple period.

The chapter is framed by a call to God to "consider" (literally "remember") (v. 1) and the realization that he continues to "ignore" (literally "forget") his people (v. 20). The body of the chapter can best be read as a portrait of occupation and the deprivation, humiliation, and frustration that accompany it. We hear the story of the survivors, the Judeans who stayed behind and who are now ruled by a foreign power (Moskowitz). That story is about the breakdown of the social, economic, political, and religious structures of Judah. Verses 2–10 portray economic impoverishment on the personal level, as it affected individuals and their families. Inherited land was taken by those outside the line of inheritance, families were bereft of the head of the household, basic products—once cheap and readily available—became expensive, and all one's energy was required for bare subsistence. Verses 11–14 move to a higher key of lament, introducing the picture of social humiliation resulting from the violence and disrespect directed at women, princes, elders, and the youth. This is a testament to the dissolution of civil society. The disintegration of Judah reaches its pinnacle in vv. 15–19 with the loss of the king and the temple—the symbols of nationhood—signaling the political and religious demise of the country.

Yet God endures and the belief in his power persists. The poem calls on God to reinstate his former relationship with Judah, but it ends in disappointment and frustration, for God is still angry with his people and continues to reject them (vv. 20–22). This chapter, like the others before it, does not resolve the problem of how Israel can find comfort after the destruction. It remains for the postexilic prophets like Second Isaiah to offer comfort and to assure their listeners that God is ready to take back his people.

Unlike the first four chapters of the book, chapter 5 does not contain an alphabetic acrostic. It does, though, have twenty-two verses, the same number as the letters of the alphabet. Most commentators, when making this observation, seem to imply that the chapter was fashioned to conform in length to the other chapters of the book. This may be so, but on the other hand, there are among the psalms chapters that contain twenty-two verses (Pss 33 and 103) and many that contain twenty-one or twenty-three verses (e.g., Pss 34, 38, 49). So the number of verses in Lam 5 may be coincidental. The verses are shorter than those in chapters 1, 2, and 4, and each falls neatly into two balanced halves, making the rhythm 3+3 instead of the 3+2 rhythm associated with laments. The balanced lines also let the parallelisms stand out clearly. The relationship of this chapter to the preceding ones is uncertain. Many commentators consider it a coda, a reprise of the thoughts of the four chapters before it, and a poetic closure to the collection as a whole.

[5:1] The poem begins with an invocation, "Consider, LORD," as the speaker representing the community tries to attract God's attention to the degraded condition of the people of Judah, which is spelled out in the following verses. The verb *zkr* ("consider"), often translated as "remember," is not a plea for God to remember something that he forgot, but to pay attention to what he is ignoring. Its opposite, *škḥ* ("to forget"), means "to ignore" (v. 20).

[2–3] The first thing mentioned on the list of losses is the disintegration of the family, the fundamental social unit in ancient Israel. The disintegration results from, and is symbolized by, the loss of inheritance (landholdings) and of the head of the household, indicating that family stability and family continuity have been undermined. In ancient Israel, great pains were taken to ensure that land was not alienated from its original owner, family, or tribe (cf. Lev 25:25–28; Num 27; 36; 1 Kgs 21:3). Thus, being deprived of one's "ancestral land" is more than a financial loss; it is a deeply felt religious or cultural loss as well, and it signifies the breakdown of society and the breakdown of God's laws.

The reference to "ancestral land" (*naḥălâ*) may carry a second nuance since *naḥălâ* is used not only for private landholdings, but for the country as a whole, the patrimony that God gave to Israel (cf. Deut 4:21). Compare Jer 12:7, where God says: "I have forsaken my *bayit* [the temple], I have abandoned my *naḥălâ* [the land]." The loss of individual land, which seems to be the plain sense of v. 2, becomes a metaphor for the loss of the country.

*naḥălâ* is paralleled by *bayit*, which can mean "house, dwelling," but here is better taken not as the physical structure but as the household, including slaves and family members. The same meaning obtains in Jer 6:12, where *bayit* parallels "fields and wives."

The other set of parallel words in v. 2 is "outsiders" (*zārîm*) and "foreigners" (*nokrîm*). While in the same semantic range, the two words are not synonymous. *zārîm* means those not belonging to the group in question (in Num 3:10 *zār* refers to a nonpriest; in 1 Kgs 3:18 it refers to people outside the prostitutes' household). An "outsider" in respect to land inheritance would be anyone not in the legitimate line of inheritance. *nokrîm* means a non-Israelite or non-Judean, so the outrageousness of the loss is extended even further. Through the use of escalating word associations (parallel word pairs), the meaning of the second line of the parallelism intensifies the meaning of the first: *ancestral land*

*// households; outsiders // foreigners.* Not only is our land taken but also our households; not only by nonfamily members but by foreigners. (Verse 11 uses the same technique of intensification in its two sets of associated words: *women // maidens; Zion // cities of Judah.*) Verse 2 is the realization of the warning in Deut 28:30–33 about the loss of possessions and family to the foreign enemy. Even closer in language to v. 2 is Esarhaddon's Succession Treaty, lines 429–30: "may your sons not take possession of your house, but a strange enemy divide your goods."[1]

Verses 2–3 show a progression from inherited land to household to father (head of household). The implication goes beyond the fact that individual land-holdings and family members have been lost; it says that the most basic elements of the social structure—the family unit and the mechanism for preserving its continuity through inheritance—have been wiped out. Verses 2 and 3 are saying that there are no patrimonies and no fathers.

Orphans and widows are among those members of society (along with the poor and the resident aliens) who have no one to protect their interests. Chayim Cohen has made a good case that *'almānâ* does not merely mean a woman who has lost her husband, but "a once married woman who has no means of financial support and who is thus in need of special legal protection."[2] An orphan is a fatherless person.[3] Compare Exod 22:23: "Your wives will be widows and your children orphans," and Ps 109:9: "His children will be orphans and his wife a widow." The threat against one's wife and children is conventional (see also Amos 7:17), and is generally directed at the husband and father, for whom it is a dire warning. In v. 3 it is presented from the perspective of the wife and children, for it is no longer a threat but a punishment already carried out.

[4–6] The picture moves from the breakup of the family to the daily struggle for survival. Wood (firewood) and water, frequently associated terms, were the most basic and readily available commodities and were free or very cheap. (That is why wood-gatherers and water-drawers were so low on the occupational hierarchy. They provided a menial service, not a product.) But now, because of scarcity, people were forced to pay for these things, perhaps exorbitant prices. Today's rhetorical equivalent would be to say that people must pay for the air they breathe. Isaiah 55:1 shows that water was free while other foods must be purchased: "Everyone who thirsts, come to the water. And he who has no money, come, buy, and eat. Come, buy wine and milk without money and without cost." Another nuance is offered by exegetes who understand "we must pay" to mean that the Judeans have lost control of their own resources.[4]

---

1. Parpola and Watanabe, *Neo-Assyrian Treaties and Loyalty Oaths*, 46.
2. "'Widowed' City," 77.
3. Contra Renkema, "Does Hebrew *ytwm* Really Mean 'Fatherless.'"
4. Dobbs-Allsopp, *Weep*, 73–74, has a brief discussion of this motif.

The phrase in v. 5, "At our necks we are pursued," is somewhat strange. Provan equates it with the English idiom "they are breathing down our necks." A more difficult question is what the phrase refers to. If the chapter is read as a survivor's story, then this description is not of the siege and battle to take Jerusalem but of its aftermath, from the perspective of those who remained in Judah. It must refer to the treatment inflicted on the defeated survivors during the occupation of Judah by the Babylonians (see Provan and Renkema).

Some exegetes prefer to emend ʿal, "on/at our necks," to ʿōl, "yoke of our necks"—see, for example, NRSV: "with a yoke on our necks." But, as several other exegetes have already objected, one is not pursued with a yoke on one's neck. The context of this verse is not one of submission to the enemy or of forced labor, but of the conditions of occupation.[5] The people feel pursued and exhausted because they must expend so much effort merely to stay alive.

[6] This verse, too, should relate to the survivors' plight, but it seems to refer to political or military alliances, which would have to have been before the destruction.[6] The time would be even earlier if "Egypt" and "Assyria" are to be taken literally, for Assyria was long gone by 586 B.C.E.

Hillers is among those who think the reference is to a past alliance, before the destruction, while Provan raises the possibility that the verse is speaking about the people who remained in Judah after 586 and sought economic help from their neighbors. I tend to see these verses as referring to the present situation, and so would side with Provan's interpretation. But Assyria as a power was long gone, making the reference to it puzzling if taken literally. Better to understand "Assyria" as a generic reference to Mesopotamia (see Ezra 6:22). The combination of Egypt and Assyria is a conventional word association (word pair) dating from the realpolitik of an earlier era but used symbolically in the postexilic period. The pairing of the two countries is found numerous times (e.g., Jer 2:18, 36; Hos 7:11; 12:2; and in the postexilic Zech 10:10, 11). Provan raises the possibility that the Judeans who remained in Judah called upon their brothers in exile, since the combination of Egypt and Assyria represents places of exile (Isa 27:13; Hos 9:3; 11:5, 11; Zech 10:10–11). I would not take seriously the notion that the Jews in exile could help those remaining in Judah; but building on Provan's observation, I sense that Egypt and Assyria became the symbol of both false alliances and places of exile. Moreover, they form a geographical merismus: the great empires to the southwest and northeast of Israel.[7] There is a certain irony in our verse, which is saying that the Judeans were so

---

5. See Hillers; Westermann; O'Connor, *NIB*.

6. "To extend the hand" implies a formal agreement swearing allegiance, equivalent to making a promise or giving a handshake, as in Ezek 17:18 and 1 Chr 29:24 (cf. 2 Kgs 10:15; Ezra 10:19; Jer 50:15 is more problematic).

7. Grossberg, *Centripetal*, 96.

desperate that they looked to the countries that had betrayed and enslaved them in the past for help in keeping themselves alive now.

**[7–10]** The description of suffering intensifies as the physiological and psychological effects are emphasized. The survivors in Judah are living in abysmal conditions that they inherited as a result of the war and occupation. Their parents, whose sins led to the destruction, are gone (dead or exiled), but the "punishments" (the miserable conditions) have not let up. Provan notes the wordplay with v. 3; in both cases the fathers are gone and the children must cope alone. I would add that in both vv. 3 and 7 the survivors speak of themselves as the children of those who suffered the brunt of the destruction, but I view this as a literary trope, not an actual intergenerational portrait. The survivors feel orphaned. This has ramifications for the interpretation of the verse's theology, which focuses on the relationship between the speakers and their fathers.

The construction of the verse, with "our fathers" and "we" at the heads of the lines, emphasizes these subjects and the parallelism between them, but the relationship between the speakers and their fathers is ambiguous. Is it emphatic or contrastive? Additional ambiguity adheres to ʿawôn, "sin" or "punishment." Do the speakers bear the sin of their fathers or suffer their punishment? The ambiguity is, perhaps, further reinforced by the absence of the conjunctive wāw in the Kethib and its presence in the Qere.

The interpretation hinges on whether the survivors view themselves as sinful. One line of interpretation suggests that not only is the present generation guilty of its own sins (3:42; 5:16), but as the children of sinners it sees itself as part of a long chain of sinners whose sins are now being punished. Compare Jer 3:25: "We have sinned against the LORD our God, we and our fathers, from our youth until this day"; and Jer 14:20: "We acknowledge, LORD, our wickedness, the guilt of our fathers, for we sinned against you." If Lam 5:7 accords with these verses in Jeremiah, both of which admit past and present wrongdoing, then it is not a question of one generation suffering because of the sins of another, but of the heavy burden of guilt that the Judeans continued to feel. The destruction did not result only from the present generation's sins, but from the long history of accumulated sin that God could no longer leave unpunished. Earlier generations escaped punishment, but this generation did not. According to this reading, the verse is not rejecting accepted theology.

On the other hand, an alternate interpretation (at odds with 3:42 and 5:16) suggests that the present speakers, the generation of the destruction, do not view themselves as sinners and therefore feel that they are being punished (unjustly) for the sins of their ancestors. If the reforms of Josiah had been successful and the people had ceased their idolatry, those living in 586 might have thought that they themselves were not guilty of sin, and that the destruction was punishment for the sins of previous generations. The idea of one generation paying for the sins of another is found in Exod 20:5 and Jer 31:28–29, and our verse may be an acknowledgment of that principle. It may also be the beginning of a rejection of it. A more well-developed rejection is found in Ezek 18, where the prophet insists that each generation is punished for its own sins, not for the sins of its ancestors.

It seems to me that both these interpretations put too much emphasis on theology and not enough on poetic expression. They take too literally the term "fathers," making it a question of which generation deserves the blame. The point is not whether the speakers feel sinful, but that they continue to endure punishment. Some Judeans were punished for their sins by death or exile, says the verse, yet the destruction and exile were not the end of the punishment. Those remaining in Judah continue to suffer that punishment, no less than those who were killed or exiled (without reference to whether they deserved it nor not). The aftermath of the destruction is part of the punishment. The survivors equate their own experience with the experience of the destruction itself, as the chapter goes on to describe scenes that are reminiscent of, and easily confused with, war and famine.

The punishments of v. 7 are detailed in vv. 8–10, and even beyond. Judah, having lost its independence, was ruled by Babylonian officials who were "slaves" or "servants" of the king of Babylonia (cf. 2 Kgs 25:24). The term "lackey" would be a modern equivalent. Before, Judah was ruled by its own king, but now it is ruled by slaves. This signals the reversal of the proper order of things, on which see Prov 30:21–22 (cf. Isa 3:4; Eccl 10:16).

Verse 3 mentioned the high price of basic commodities, and now v. 9 describes how scarce food was and how difficult to obtain. A common translation of the verse is: "At the risk of our lives we get bread, because of the sword of the wilderness" (cf. NJPS, NRSV, NIV). "Sword of the wilderness" is a crux, and has been taken by many interpreters as a metaphoric expression for "bedouin" or "pursuers." McDaniel ("Philological Studies, I," 51–52), following Dahood, prefers "sword of the pursuer" (taking *midbār* from *dbr*, "to drive out, pursue"). The usual explanation, going back to the Targum, is that scavenging for food in the countryside was dangerous because of marauding bandits. Other exegetes emend to "heat of the wilderness," yielding a better parallel with v. 10 (reading *ḥōreb* for *ḥereb*; cf. Job 30:30 for skin blackened from the heat). But, it is not necessary to emend, for Deut 28:22 has *ḥereb* in the sense of "drought." In fact, the key to vv. 9–10 is in Deut 28:22, which warns about disease, fever, scorching heat, and drought. Those conditions of drought and disease are described, in highly metaphoric language, in vv. 9–10 as pertaining in Judah itself. There are no bandits and no wilderness; Judah itself is as dry as the wilderness (either from a natural scarcity of rain or from poor water management), and starvation and dehydration are the sword that kills. In addition to the metaphors, the words *ḥereb*, *midbār* ("wilderness"), and *rāʿāb* ("famine") play on the familiar triad *ḥereb* ("sword"), *deber* ("plague"), and *rāʿāb* ("famine"), often used in connection with war, siege, and their aftermath (see O. Kaiser, *"ḥereb," TDOT* 5:164–65). (So *ḥereb hammidbār* may have the double entendre of "sword of the plague.")

Because of the difficulty in obtaining food, malnutrition sets in and is described in v. 10. The physiological description is similar to but less extensive than the siege famine in 4:8. If my interpretation is correct, v. 10 is not the famine of the siege, but the scarcity of food resulting from the social and economic breakdown of the country.

[11–14] The enumeration of private indignities and the more pervasive and public dangers to the mental and physical well-being of the community now escalate into a recitation of the brutality against the population of Judah. The picture is of rape, torture, and inhumane labor, which constitutes physical abuse and which demoralizes the community.

I have not translated *bĕtûlâ* as "virgin" because the Hebrew term does not bear the semantic load that "virgin" does in our society. The reference is to a young woman of marriageable age.[8] The issue is not anatomical or moral, but rather the social and legal status of the woman. *ʾIššâ* may be a general designation for women or may refer to married women. The parallelism can thus be analyzed as moving from the general to the specific, from a broader to a narrower category: all women // unmarried women; or as using contrasting word associates: married women // unmarried women. (An analogous set of words is *yād* // *yāmîn*, "hand" // "right hand" in Judg 5:26.) In either case, *bĕtûlōt* is the more poignant of its pair. The parallelism of "Zion" // "cities of Judah" moves in the opposite direction, from a more specific location to a wider panorama. The effect of both sets of word associations together is to intensify the meaning. The raping occurred not only in the capital but throughout the towns of Judah, and it included women not yet married. By means of this progression, rape becomes more offensive and more widespread. Rape is the all-too-frequent concomitant to war, and is a systematic way of perpetrating violence against the population at large, not only against the fighting army. This type of violence is more than physical, for it inflicts submission and shame on its victims; and the victims of rape are also the men in society whose wives and daughters and mothers are raped.

Verse 12 continues the description of the vicious treatment and shaming received at the hands of the enemy. The expression "by their hands" is ambiguous. Does it refer to the part of the body by which the princes were hung? Compare the Annals of Ashurbanipal (*ANET,* 295): "They arrested these kings and put their hands and feet in iron cuffs and fetters." Alternatively, *bĕyādām* indicates agency, those doing the hanging. NJPS understands it as "Princes have been

---

8. Day, "Personification of Cities," 283 n. 2, assembles references to the term *bĕtûlâ*, including the suggestion that it may signify a woman between menarche and the birth of her first child.

hanged *by them.*" Hanging was not a means of execution, but the way in which a corpse was publicly displayed in order to shame the victim and his people. The reference to hanging in our verse, however, remains obscure. I agree with Provan that it is probably not execution or the display of corpses that is being meant, but a form of humiliation or torture to the living. Respect for elders is commanded in Lev 19:32. The curse in Deut 28:50 warns of a ruthless nation that will show no deference to the elders.

In the context of the preceding verses, v. 13 should also be interpreted as telling of the maltreatment of the population, in this case the heavy and demeaning labor that was forced upon the young men. The impact of pulling the millstone and bearing loads of wood is not, however, immediately apparent. Milling flour on a small hand mill was done for the family by slaves or, in small households, by women. There were in the ancient Near East larger milling operations, "milling houses," often run by the state, in which the workers were either impoverished male citizens or prisoners of war.[9] It is perhaps to the latter that our verse refers. An interesting parallel is found in an Old Babylonian letter: "He took your wife and your daughter as pledges. Come back before your wife and your daughter die from the work of constantly grinding barley while in detention."[10] Compare Job 31:10, where "May my wife grind for another" has a sexual connotation. Isaiah 47:2 says that part of Babylonia's punishment will be to take the millstone (*rēḥayim*) and grind flour. Clearly, milling was a demeaning type of labor (especially for a man), and the phrase makes sense if taken this way. However, this interpretation does not account for "pulling" (*nāśā'*) the millstone, an unusual usage. So I propose another interpretation— one that more closely parallels the second line—namely that young men, rather than animals, must pull the millstone that grinds the grain. Large rotary mills pulled by donkeys are known by the Hellenistic period, although whether they were used earlier is questionable. If the reference is indeed to a large rotary mill, we have here the picture of young men doing the work of animals. This idea is also found in the second line. Loads of wood would normally be carried on a donkey, but here they are carried on the backs of young men or boys. In the basic "industries" necessary to sustain the community, exemplified by grinding flour and providing fuel, people are worked like animals. These actions, like those in vv. 11–12, have both a physical and a psychological effect on the victims.

Verse 14 is a transition verse. It shows the result of the maltreatment mentioned before, which is that old and young are gone from the public places where they used to gather and from the public activities they used to engage in. That is to say, there is no more public life, no normal civic activities. The "gate"

9. K. van der Torn, "Mill, Millstone," *ABD* 4:831–32.
10. *UET* 59, translated in A. L. Oppenheim, *Letters from Mesopotamia* (Chicago: University of Chicago Press, 1967), 91.

refers to the city gate, the place where the elders congregated and where business was conducted (Prov 31:23; Ruth 4:1–2). Music signifies public celebrations. Verse 14 also segues into the idea of cessation expressed by "gone" (*šābat*) in vv. 14 and 15. The sense of loss that derives from the cessation of everything normal is prominent in the chapter as a whole.

[15–19] These verses move into the public, or institutional, domain. The loss of the king and the temple are the climax of the list of losses in the chapter. They represent the loss of the nation qua nation, and the dissolution of the Davidic covenant.

Verse 15, which follows naturally from v. 14, does not refer merely to the absence of music in the city streets. It is a reference to the cessation of temple worship (Ibn Ezra, based on the word *māśôś* in Ezek 24:25). "The joy (*māśôś*) of our heart" refers to the Temple Mount, "the joy of the whole land" (Lam 2:15; Ps 48:3). The word *māḥôl*, "rejoicing," is associated with dancing or instrumental music, and here refers to the festive celebrations at the temple, which have now been transformed into lamentations for its loss. Joy is not a state of mind but a ritual experience performed in the presence of God, while mourning signals the absence of God.[11]

The crown in v. 16 symbolizes honor (Isa 28:1, 3; Job 19:9), but more than that it symbolizes *kingship*, for it is the fall of the Davidic monarchy that is being lamented here, along with the destruction of the temple ("the joy of our heart" in v. 15). Dobbs-Allsopp (*NOAB*, 1178 Hebrew Bible) sees a more physical image, noting: "The crenellated walls of Palestinian cities were often likened to great crowns adorning the head of the city (Isa 28:1–5; 54:11; Jer 13:18; Ezek 16:12; Mic 4:8)."[12] The destruction of the temple and the end of the monarchy are the reasons that hearts languish and eyes have lost their brightness. Notice that parts of the body—hearts, heads, eyes—are used to register the impact of the destruction. The words "heart" and "eyes" (v. 17) are an associated pair.[13] The antecedents of "this" and "these" (v. 17) are not clear but may be in the next verse: the temple and the foxes (see 3:21 for a proleptic "this"). The prolepsis seems likely because the first word in v. 18 is the same as the first word in each line of v. 17. On the other hand, it is not necessary to look for specific referents as "this" and "these" may refer to everything described. The pairing of singular and plural in parallelism is not uncommon.[14]

Verse 18 makes explicit what was implicit in the preceding verses, namely, that the temple is destroyed. Following NRSV, NJPS, and others, I construe the first word of v. 18, *ʿal*, as having the same meaning as the first word of the pre-

---

11. Anderson, *Time to Mourn*, 107–9.
12. For more on mural crowns see Biddle, "The Figure of Lady Jerusalem," especially 178–86.
13. W. Watson, "The Unnoticed Word Pair."
14. See Berlin, *Dynamics*, 44–50.

ceding verse, "because of." Hillers and Provan take it as "on," rendering the verse: "On Mount Zion, which lies desolate, foxes prowl about." Imagery of foxes around ruins is found in the Curse of Agade, line 257: "May foxes that frequent ruined mounds sweep with their tails."[15]

Verse 19 makes an important theological statement. God remains enthroned forever even though his throne, the temple, is physically destroyed. God is not physically or spatially limited to his temple, and his existence does not depend on a physical structure. Nor can he be carried off like the statues of pagan gods were when their countries were conquered. A comparison with the almost identical Ps 102:13 is instructive. Psalm 102:13 differs from our verse in only one word: "You, LORD, are enthroned forever, your *zeker* ('name/fame') is everlasting." The psalm uses the parallelism to emphasize God's permanence and power, upon which the psalmist calls for help. ("You" contrasts the permanence of God with the transience of the psalmist.) Our verse, on the other hand, emphasizes God's sitting on his throne, contrasting its physical ruin with its theological permanence, as if to say: The temple may be destroyed but God's throne is indestructible. As Isa 57:15 puts it, God dwells forever, he dwells on high. See Pss 9:7 and 29:10 for similar expressions of God's eternal presence. The contrast between God and the destroyed temple is strengthened by the syntax, which places the independent pronoun "you" at the head of v. 19 (Hillers). Although there is no conjunctive particle, NJPS and NRSV translate "But you, LORD."

[20–22] The idea that God exists separate from the temple should bring hope to the Judeans that he will aid them, but this hope is dashed immediately by God's refusal to respond. The plea to "remember" or consider the people's plight in v. 1 goes unheeded; God continues to "forget" or ignore them. Just as God exists forever, so his abandonment of Israel goes on forever, or so it seems to our poet. (For similar language see Ps 74:1.) Isaiah 54:7–8, in words of comfort, reverses the proportion of time, making God's anger and rejection of short duration and his mercy never-ending. Verse 21 pleads that the former relationship between God and the people may be reinstated; but v. 22 ends the prayer on a note of despair and a feeling of permanent rejection. The last chapter, and with it the book as a whole, fail to provide the comfort that has been sought throughout it. The book thereby remains a perpetual lament commemorating unconsolable mourning.

[22] I take the words "But instead" (*kî ʾim*) in a restrictive sense, in opposition to what went before. The meaning of the phrase has been debated in the commentaries. Linafelt proposes a novel solution. He separates the two words instead of seeing them as an idiom, and translates: "For if truly you have rejected us, bitterly raged against us. . . ." He leaves the last verse unfinished, trailing off. In his words, "The book is left opening out into the emptiness of

15. Cooper, *Curse of Agade*, 63.

God's nonresponse."[16] This interpretation may resonate with the modern reader, but it is likely too modern for the ancient author.

In Jewish tradition the custom in public recitation is to repeat the penultimate verse when a book ends on a negative note, as here and also in Isaiah, Malachi, and Ecclesiastes, so as not to conclude on a note of despair. This provides the positive closure that is expected and that is found in most other biblical books.

16. *Surviving Lamentations*, 60.

# Index of Authors

# Index of Scripture and Other Ancient Literature

## APOCRYPHA

## DEAD SEA SCROLLS—QUMRAM LITERATURE

Lightning Source UK Ltd.
Milton Keynes UK
UKOW01f0430190117
292289UK00001B/31/P